News That Matters

AMERICAN POLITICS AND POLITICAL ECONOMY
Benjamin I. Page, Series Editor

NEWS THAT MATTERS

Television and American Opinion

Shanto Iyengar and Donald R. Kinder

THE UNIVERSITY OF CHICAGO PRESS
CHICAGO AND LONDON

SHANTO IYENGAR is associate professor of political
science at the State University of New York, Stony Brook.
DONALD R. KINDER is professor of political science
and psychology at the University of Michigan.

The University of Chicago Press, Chicago 60637
The University of Chicago Press, Ltd., London

Library of Congress Cataloging-in-Publication Data
Iyengar, Shanto.
  News that matters.

  (American politics and political economy)
  Bibliography: p.
  Includes index.
  1. Television broadcasting of news—Political
aspects—United States.   2. Television broadcasting
of news—United States—Psychological aspects.
3. Television and politics—United States.
4. Public opinion—United States.   I. Kinder,
Donald R.   II. Title.
PN4888.T4I94   1987   302.2′345   86-30845
ISBN 0-226-38856-5

Contents

Acknowledgments

This book is the product of an extended collaboration that began at Yale University in 1979 and ended, thanks only to the miracle of word processing, about five minutes ago with Iyengar in Stony Brook and Kinder in Palo Alto. Along this long road, we incurred many debts.

In the early days, when we were not yet fully persuaded that the political effects of television could be studied usefully by experimental means, Robert Abelson and William McGuire provided essential and much appreciated encouragement. Since then, many people have offered advice. Much of it was enlightened; some of it we took. For wading through early versions of the book, red pencils in hand, we would like to thank Edie Goldenberg, Michael MacKuen, Warren Miller, Benjamin Page, Ellen Robb, and Janet Weiss. Don Herzog, Samuel Popkin, and Steven Rosenstone went far beyond the call of collegial duty. Their detailed and thoughtful reactions improved the book and enriched our understanding of our own work. We hope someday to return the favor.

We were also blessed with exceptional graduate student assistants. At Yale, Mark Peters and Roy Behr not only managed the running of our experiments but also contributed significantly to our thinking about television and politics. We are particularly grateful to Behr for allowing us to use a portion of his dissertation research. At Michigan, Jon Krosnick was a tireless analyst and kibitzer whose relentless questioning strengthened the work (and, in time, our friendship).

Our experiments necessitated the use of sophisticated audiovisual facilities and equipment. The late Frank Dendas, director of the Yale Television Studio, gave generously of his time and expertise, and welcomed us to the Studio's remarkable facilities. Lawrence Grippo, then a Yale undergraduate, skillfully "created" our newscasts, somehow kept track of our overflowing collection of videotapes, and ably assisted in the running of experiments. We would also like to thank the hundreds of people in New Haven and Ann Arbor who saw fit to participate in our studies. Without their cooperation, this book could not have been written. As chair of the department of political science at Yale, David Mayhew helped us find necessary resources. We are also grateful to

Nancy Brennan at the Center for Political Studies at Michigan and Estelle Krieger at the department of political science at Stony Brook for preparing the manuscript—again and again, with great cheer and competence.

Over the years, our research was funded by grants from the political science program at the National Science Foundation (Grants SES 80-12581, 81-21306, and 82-08714). We thank program directors Gerald Wright and Frank Scioli for ably shepherding our proposals through the Foundation. Additional support came from the National Institutes of Health (in the form of a postdoctoral fellowship to Iyengar) and the Block Fund of Yale University. Most of the national survey data we report were made available by the Inter-University Consortium for Political and Social Research. They were originally collected by the Center for Political Studies (CPS) of the Institute for Social Research, the University of Michigan, for the National Election Studies. Neither CPS nor the Consortium bears any responsibility for the analyses or interpretations we offer here. Nor does anybody else. In the spirit of true collaboration, we have only each other to blame.

Last, but hardly least, we wish to express our gratitude to our spouses and our children. Were it not for Ellen and Nikhil, and Janet and Benjamin, we would no doubt have completed this project sooner, but would have been unimaginably poorer for it.

A Primordial Power?

On a typical weekday evening, some fifty million Americans gather around their television sets, tuned into the national newscasts of the three major networks. By a wide margin, they believe that television—not magazines, not radio, not newspapers—provides the most intelligent, complete, and impartial coverage of public affairs, and goes furthest in clarifying the candidacies and issues at stake in national elections (Bower 1985). We Americans trust television news; we see it as authoritative (perhaps in part because we *see* it); we have welcomed Huntley, Cronkite, Brokaw, and the others into our living rooms gladly.

Because of its wide reach and high credibility, television news obviously possesses the potential to shape American public opinion profoundly. Whether television news realizes this potential, however, is the subject of considerable and occasionally acrimonious debate. In fact, research has more often than not concluded that mass media in general and television news in particular merely strengthen or reinforce the public's existing beliefs and opinions.[1] Indeed, Patterson and McClure (1976) concluded that television news coverage of presidential campaigns had virtually no political impact. According to their analysis, network news failed even to *inform* voters regarding the choices they confronted. Why? Patterson and McClure put it this way: "Since the nightly news is too brief to treat fully the complexity of modern politics, too visual to present effectively most events, and too entertainment-minded to tell viewers much worth knowing, most network newscasts are neither very educational nor very powerful communicators" (1976, 90).

We subscribe to much of this indictment. Television news is brief; it does drastically simplify the complexity of modern politics; it is undeniably visual; and it does borrow unabashedly from the world of entertainment television. We know, moreover, that viewers typically pay rather casual and intermittent attention to the parade of stories that make up the news each night (Kinder and Sears 1985, 660–64).

Nevertheless, we believe that Patterson and McClure's conclusion—that "network newscasts are neither very educational nor very powerful communicators"—is quite thoroughly mistaken. Our purpose here is to establish that television news is in fact an educator virtually without peer, that it shapes the American public's conception of political life in pervasive ways; that television news is news that matters.

Our argument begins with the observation that Americans develop opinions toward an astonishing variety of issues that lie far outside their own experience. To be sure, they are preoccupied first and foremost with the immediate concerns of private life: with earning a living, supporting a family, making and keeping friends. But at the same time, they also manage to decide whether huge federal deficits threaten the economy and whether fighting in Latin America threatens national security. They reach such judgments without benefit of direct experience: without undertaking their own economic analysis, without traveling behind the lines in Nicaragua. Because they take part in the grand events of politics so rarely, ordinary Americans must depend upon information and analysis provided by others—in modern times, upon information and analysis provided by mass media.

This dependence gives the media an enormous capacity to shape public thinking. Cohen has put this point well, and although he was writing with newspapers in mind, his argument applies with at least equal force to television news:

The press is significantly more than a purveyor of information and opinion. It may not be successful much of the time in telling people what to think, but it is stunningly successful in telling its readers what to think *about*. And it follows from this that the world looks different to different people, depending not only on their personal interests, but also on the map that is drawn for them by the writers, editors, and publishers of the papers they read. Perhaps the notion of a map is too confining, for it does not suggest the full range of the political phenomena that are conveyed by the press. It is, more properly, an atlas of places, personages, situations, and events; and to the extent that the press even discusses the ideas that men have for coping with the day's ration of problems, it is an atlas of policy possibilities, alternatives, choices. The editor may believe he is only printing the things that people want to read, but he is thereby putting a claim on their attention, powerfully determining what they will be thinking about, and talking about, until the next wave laps their shore (1963, 13).

While agenda-setting—to adopt the social science parlance—has been the subject of thoughtful essays over the last half century,[2] empirical work on the subject has a briefer and less distinguished history. Lippmann's (1920, 1922, 1925) original warning that news organizations possess the power to determine what the public takes to be important had little immediate impact on research. Even forty years later, Klapper's encyclopedic summary of findings on the effects of mass communication could devote just two pages to agenda-setting; moreover, that discussion was dotted with such disheartening phrases as "it is a matter of common observation" or "some writers believe" (1960, 104–5). Although research on agenda-setting has proliferated over the last decade, so far, unfortunately, the results add up to rather little.[3] Even exponents of the agenda-setting idea acknowledge the literature's fragmented and haphazard condition (e.g., McCombs 1981). Agenda-setting may be an apt metaphor, but it is no theory.

The lack of a theory of media effects has significantly impeded our understanding of how democracy works. The health and vitality of any democratic government depend in part on the wisdom of ordinary citizens. And indeed, commentaries on the current state of the American polity, in scholarly journals and on the editorial page, are laced with normative claims that the public is or is not rational, that the American citizen is shrewd or foolish. Such claims typically pay no attention whatsoever to the dissemination of political information throughout society, to the no-doubt intricate relationship that has grown up between the institutions of mass communication, on the one hand, and the political wisdom of ordinary citizens, on the other. Lippmann was not exaggerating the political significance of this relationship when he wrote that citizens "who have lost their grip upon the relevant facts of their environment are the inevitable victims of agitation and propaganda. The quack, the charlatan, the jingo, and the terrorist can flourish only where the audience is deprived of independent access to information" (1920, 54–55). If we are to understand and assess how well the American political system works, surely we need a theory of how information about public affairs percolates through American society.

We begin to develop such a theory here, as part of our effort to understand the ways in which television news shapes the political thinking of ordinary Americans. We test and refine our understanding mainly—though not exclusively—with experiments, a powerful method of investigation that media researchers have largely ignored. Our fourteen experiments introduce systematic and unobtrusive alterations into the television news broadcasts that ordinary citizens watch. As a consequence, citizens assigned to different experimental conditions are furnished with slightly different glimpses of the political world— and as we will see, such differences matter greatly. Because our procedures are unusual, we explain them fully in chapter 2. There we define exactly what we mean by an experiment, argue that experimentation possesses distinctive strengths for the study of television news, and then describe the particular experimental designs we deployed in our research.

Chapter 3 presents results from a series of experiments on agenda-setting, supplemented at key junctures with complementary evidence drawn from our analysis of national surveys. Taken together, the results vindicate Lippmann's original suspicion that news media provide compelling accounts of a political world that is otherwise out of reach. Our studies show specifically that *television news powerfully influences which problems viewers regard as the nation's most serious.* Rising prices, unemployment, energy shortages, arms control—all these (and more) become high priority political issues for the public only if they first become high priority news items for the networks.

In chapter 4 we examine characteristics of coverage that might accentuate the agenda-setting effect. We compare stories that lead off the evening news with those that appear later in the broadcast, on the hypothesis that lead stories might be more influential merely because of their position. (They are.) We also assess whether the dramatic personal vignettes that the networks commonly use to illustrate national problems, which are surely riveting, are also particularly influential. (They are not.)

In chapter 5 we examine how television's portrayal of national problems interacts with viewers' personal circumstances. Racial discrimination, job loss, and the threatened collapse of the social security system (among others) are national problems and, for some Americans, overwhelming personal ones as well. Do such direct experiences override the vicarious experiences provided by television news? (They do not.) In chapter 6 we investigate several characteristics of viewers that might make them more or less vulnerable to agenda-setting. We compare the reactions of the well-educated and the poorly-educated, partisans and independents, the politically involved and the politically withdrawn, thereby hoping to identify more precisely just who is affected by agenda-setting.

Chapters 7 through 11 take up what we call "priming," a manifestation of television power that is more insidious and perhaps more consequential than agenda-setting. Priming presumes that when evaluating complex political objects—the performance of an incumbent president, or the promises of a presidential contender—citizens do not take into account all that they know. They cannot, even if they were motivated to do so. What they do consider is what comes to mind, those bits and pieces of political memory that are accessible. And television news, we argue, is a most powerful force determining what springs to the citizen's mind and what does not. *By priming certain aspects of national life while ignoring others, television news sets the terms by which political judgments are rendered and political choices made.*

Chapter 7 discusses the impact of priming on citizens' evaluations of the president's performance. When primed by television news stories that focus on national defense, citizens judge the president largely by how well he has provided, as they see it, for the nation's defense; when primed by stories about inflation, citizens evaluate the president by how well he has managed, in their view, to keep prices down; and so on. In chapter 8, we explore whether priming also influences the judgments the public renders regarding the president's *character*. (It does, in complex and interesting ways.) In chapter 9, we investigate whether the magnitude of the priming effect depends on how deeply the news implicates government, and especially on what we term the level of presidential responsibility implicit in television news coverage. (It does.) Chapter 10 then does for priming what chapter 6 did for agenda-setting: there we identify who is especially vulnerable to priming and discover to our surprise that the victims of priming are not the same people who are the victims of agenda-setting. In chapter 11, to complete the empirical work, we describe two experiments that concentrate on the electoral consequence of priming. There we show that the priorities that are uppermost in voters' minds when they go to the polls are powerfully shaped by the last-minute preoccupations of television news.

In chapter 12, we tie the various results together, conclude that, like it or not, television news has become a serious and relentless player in the American political process, and, finally, take up the claim that television news conveys unusual and distinctive views of American politics, under the assumption, handsomely supported by our research, that such views eventually become our own.

Pathways to Knowledge: Experimentation and the Analysis of Television's Power

The word "experiment" means many things, not only to the proverbial person in the street, but to social scientists as well. Consequently, it is important for us to be clear at the outset about what we mean—and do not mean—by experiment. For us, the essence of the true experiment is control. Experiments of the sort we have undertaken here are distinguished from other systematic empirical methods in the special measure of control they give to the investigator. In the first place, the experimenter *creates* the conditions under investigation, rather than waiting for them to occur naturally. In the second place, the experimenter *randomly assigns* individuals to those conditions, thereby superseding natural processes of selection. By creating the conditions of interest, the experimenter holds extraneous factors constant and ensures that individuals will encounter conditions that differ only in theoretically decisive ways. By assigning individuals to conditions randomly, the experimenter can be confident that any resulting differences between individuals assigned to varying conditions must be caused by differences in the conditions themselves.

Although these features may seem innocuous, they are not: experiments possess genuine advantages over alternative approaches, particularly in the insight they provide into causation. Because this claim may appear pretentious, we will try to illustrate it with a simple example.

Suppose (as is true) that we are interested in the influence television news might exercise over the American public. Like many researchers before us, we therefore decide to interview a sample of Americans, carefully selected to be representative of the nation as a whole. We partition our sample into two groups, those who tell us that they rely primarily upon television news for their information about politics and those who say they rely on other sources. We then compare the political views of the two groups and discover that the television-reliant group regards unemployment as the country's most serious problem while the other group names inflation. Simultaneously, we undertake a content analysis of television news coverage, finding that during the period of our interviews, television news has been preoccupied with unemployment. We conclude that television news does indeed shape its viewers' conceptions of political reality.

There is nothing wildly foolish about this hypothetical study. It does have serious limitations, however, just those that a true experiment counteracts. First and foremost, our hypothetical study cannot establish causal relationships. Observing that television news coverage and viewers' beliefs correspond is not the same as establishing that television coverage influences viewers' beliefs. No doubt the television-reliant group differs in many ways from those who obtain their information elsewhere, and it may be these differences that are responsible for generating different outlooks on national problems. If the television group is disproportionately working-class, for example, their special concern about unemployment might be due not to television coverage but to their own experiences in the labor force, or the experiences of their friends and coworkers. Of course, we might be able to test this particular explanation by partitioning the sample into different occupational groups and then examining whether the same relationship between television viewing and political outlook was maintained within each occupational group. But we could never know for certain whether *all* such plausible rival explanations had been ruled out.

This limitation of nonexperimental research is debilitating for causal inference, and it is exactly the problem overcome in experimentation through random assignment. By randomly assigning some people to television and others to newspapers (ignoring for the moment any ethical and practical difficulties that might stand in the way), the experimenter can be certain that whatever differences are detected between the two groups can be traced to differences in the treatments. Alternative explanations due to preexposure differences—associated with class, unemployment experiences, *or anything else*—are made untenable by this simple procedure.

Suppose we could, through some miracle of omniscience, rule out all plausible rival interpretations for our survey result. We would then know that television's agenda influenced the public—but little more than that. We could only speculate about which characteristics of television news are responsible for shaping public opinion. This limitation highlights another advantage of experimentation. By creating treatment and control conditions, the experimenter can isolate one causal variable at a time, thereby opening the way for a more refined understanding of how television influences its audience. Unlike the survey analyst, the experimenter need not wait for history to provide crucial tests.

Despite these advantages, true experiments are few and far between in the study of politics. There are notable exceptions: Gosnell's (1927) studies of voter turnout in Chicago more than a half-century ago (also see Eldersveld 1956); Campbell's (1969b) advocacy of an experimental approach to evaluating social reforms; and recent experiments on political bargaining and committee decision-making (e.g., Fiorina and Plott 1978). But by and large, students of politics have been reluctant to intervene experimentally in natural political processes. We suffer no such hesitation; we move ahead, confident that experiments bestow advantages unattainable by other means.

THE EXPERIMENTAL DESIGNS[1]

OVERVIEW

All our experiments were advertised as studies of citizens' reactions to television news programs and followed one of two basic designs. In *sequential* experiments, participants were exposed to a sequence of unobtrusively altered network newscasts. Participants viewed one thirty-minute newscast every day over the course of one week. On the experiment's first day, participants came to a building on the campus of Yale University and were instructed concerning the objectives and procedures of the study. They were told that it was necessary for them to watch the news at the University in order to avoid distractions present at home and to ensure that everyone watched the same broadcasts under identical conditions, and that during the length of the experiment they should *not* watch the evening national news at home. They then completed a questionnaire that covered a variety of political topics. Most germane to our interest in agenda-setting and priming, participants were asked to name the country's most important problems and to evaluate the president's performance in office. After completing the questionnaire, participants were shown an unedited videotape recording of the previous evening's national newscast drawn from one of the three major networks. Over the next four days, participants continued to view what they believed to be simply a recording of the previous evening's network newscast. In fact, unknown to participants, we had altered sections of the newscast ahead of time in order to achieve systematic experimental variations in the amount and nature of coverage given national problems. In experiment 2, for example, participants randomly assigned to one condition received a steady dose of news alleging inadequacies in United States defense capability; a second group watched newscasts that paid special attention to pollution; a third group saw newscasts that emphasized economic problems. Each condition was characterized not only by sustained coverage of the target problem (e.g., defense), but also by systematic exclusion of news stories dealing with the other two (pollution and the economy). Thus each condition served as a control group for the others. On the final (sixth) day of the experiment, participants completed a second questionnaire that again inquired into their beliefs about the country's problems and the president's performance.

In *assemblage* experiments, in contrast, participants viewed a collection of news stories taken from the three networks at a single sitting—in different studies, as few as eight stories to as many as thirteen. The presentations were described as a cross-section of typical news stories broadcast by the major networks during the past year. As in sequential designs, the presentations in assemblage experimentations were put together in order to test propositions about agenda-setting and priming. Immediately after the presentations—and *only* afterwards, in contrast to sequential experiments—participants were questioned about their political views.

Although the assemblage design simulates less faithfully the ordinary American's encounters with television news than does its sequential counterpart, it does have one decisive advantage. Because assemblage treatment conditions can be prepared well in advance of the running of the experiment itself, they can be calibrated precisely. Hence assemblage experiments are particularly useful for testing relatively subtle ideas about how television might work its influence. Experiment 3, for example, examined whether priming is enhanced when television news both pays substantial attention to a problem and implies that the president is responsible for the problem. Participants in this experiment saw either many stories describing America's growing dependence on foreign oil or only a few; moreover, the stories implied either that the president had a great deal to do with the nation's energy problems or that the causes of and solutions for the country's energy predicament lay elsewhere. Crossing the two factors—exposure and responsibility—results in four experimental treatments. (Participants in a fifth, control, condition saw no stories about energy at all.)

In summary, participants in sequential experiments viewed unobtrusively edited newscasts over the course of a week. In assemblage experiments, participants watched a single collection of news stories in one session. The assemblage design is obviously less realistic, but in partial compensation, it enables us to pursue more subtle propositions regarding the power of television news. As a general strategy we deployed the two designs together hoping to take advantage of their complementary strengths.

We recruited experimental participants by placing advertisements in local newspapers and by displaying posters in various public locations. The notices promised payment in return for participating in research on television news (typically $20 for sequential experiments and $7 for assemblage experiments). When individuals responded to the advertisements, we obtained information about their demographic characteristics (so as to exclude students, noncitizens, and those under the age of eighteen). Participants selected one of several daily viewing sessions; we then randomly assigned sessions to experimental condition.

A critical feature of both experimental designs is the creation of realistic newscasts. Because the procedure is more elaborate for sequential experiments, we will describe it in some detail. On the evening prior to each session, we videotaped the national newscasts of two of the major networks. To create slightly different broadcasts for each experimental condition, we then edited the actual newscast. We inserted stories into the newscasts, meanwhile deleting innocuous material of roughly equivalent length. The stories we inserted had been broadcast six to eight months earlier by the same network. We made certain that these stories contained no clues as to their actual date of broadcast by selecting feature stories that were relatively "timeless." (In many cases, these stories were themselves edited in order to remove temporal markers.) To do so we accumulated a large pool of news stories, dealing with ten separate problems, from the Vanderbilt University Television News Archive and from the audiovisual facilities at Yale University. For each network and for each problem, we compiled stories from several different reporters introduced by different anchorpersons. Some were winter stories and others were summer stories; some implicated the president and others did not; some displayed "talking heads" while others featured dramatic action. In short, on any given day, we had a large and diverse pool of potential stories from which to draw.

The treatment story (usually one each day) was inserted during the middle portion of the newscast and usually ran for two to four minutes. In practice the actual newscast was left substantially intact except for the insertion of the treatment story and the deletion of a story or two in compensation. Over the course of a typical sequential experiment, a treatment consisted of four implanted stories spread across four days, totaling about twelve minutes of news time (treatments ranged from seven to seventeen minutes of total coverage). From the networks' point of view, this level of attention represents a substantial commitment, but not an extraordinary one. During 1985, for example, the federal deficit, various hijackings, the crisis in Lebanon, the Nicaraguan conflict, the summit meeting between President Reagan and Secretary General Gorbachev, all drew at least as much weekly coverage as did our experimental problems. It would have been easy, and not particularly interesting, to demonstrate television effects by overwhelming our participants with an avalanche of stories about one problem or another. Such a demonstration would tell us about the potential power of television under extraordinary circumstances. Our interest rather is in the real power of television under ordinary circumstances, and so we designed our experimental treatments to fall within television news's normal range.

AVOIDING EXPERIMENTAL ARTIFACTS

In any experimental procedure it is important to guard against "demand characteristics"—cues in the setting that suggest to participants what is expected of them (Orne 1962). In order to limit the impact of demand characteristics in our experiments, we undertook several precautions. First, we disguised the purpose of our experiments. We began both sequential and assemblage experiments by presenting to participants an entirely plausible but false account of our purpose. Participants were informed that the study was about how people interpret and understand television news and that we were particularly interested in "what social scientists call selective perception. Do viewers' political opinions color what they see in the news? Do Republicans and Democrats really see the same news story?" Because this description provided a compelling explanation for what the participants were in fact later asked to do—namely, reveal their political opinions and evaluate news stories—we hoped it would discourage them from wondering what we were really doing.

Second, to lessen their prominence, we embedded our key measures of problem importance and presidential performance in a lengthy questionnaire. In addition to these questions of real interest, we also asked participants for their opinions on current issues, their explanations for the nation's problems, their perceptions of an ideal president, their partisan leanings, their recent political activities, and so forth.

We believe our precautions were successful. At the conclusion of each study (after the questionnaires had been collected and the participants paid), all participants were asked to describe their perceptions of what the experiment was about now that they had completed it, and whether their perceptions were consistent with their initial expectations. Across all our experiments, only a handful of participants expressed any skepticism about what we were up to—and most of these skeptics supposed that we were actually engaged in market research for the networks.

Finally, after learning what we could about our participants' perceptions of our purpose, we then gently revealed our real purposes to them. We told them that we had altered the newscasts and described how and why we had done so. We tried to explain the value of their participation to our understanding of the political effects of television news. Participants who indicated interest in our work were sent copies of our papers. We regard this "debriefing" as an essential part of our experiments. As a general matter, our procedures adhered scrupulously to the American Psychological Association's guidelines governing the protection of human subjects in experimental research.

METHODOLOGICAL PLURALISM

Experiments have their limitations, of course, which ours do not avoid. While experiments are uniquely strong on matters of *internal validity,* providing evidence on causal relationships, they are typically weak on matters of *external validity,* providing assurance about the generalizability of results. Naturally, we seek generalizable results. The various experimental findings reported in the chapters to come are of interest only insofar as they bear on the workings of television news and public opinion in their natural settings. But to generalize from our experimental arrangements and populations to the American living room and ordinary Americans is to participate in what Campbell (1969a) has called "the scandal of induction." Generalizations always entail a leap of faith; even if informed, they are inescapably matters of opinion.

Concern about the generalizability of experimental results usually takes three principal forms. First, because experimental participants ordinarily know that they are taking part in the study of something (even if they're not sure what), this knowledge alone may induce alterations in their behavior. They might become more attentive; they might become less. They might defer to the experimenter's authority; they might react against it. Each represents a response to the special and in some respects *artificial* nature of the research setting. Second, experiments are often conducted with populations of convenience. Because convenient populations are often special populations, such practice has naturally led to skepticism regarding whether experimental results can be safely generalized to populations of real interest. For social scientists stationed at universities, no population is of course more convenient than the student body. And the typical college sophomore, as Hovland (1959) warned some years ago, may be very far from typical of the average adult American. Third, experimental results are always subject to the charge that they depend precariously on exactly how the variables under investigation are created or measured. Perhaps an intriguing result would simply disappear in another experiment, with conditions realized or questions posed in slightly different ways. Results that conform neatly to expectations in one experiment may become inexplicable in another.

These threats to the external validity of experimental results—whether they can be generalized across settings, populations, independent and dependent variables—can certainly be raised with respect to our experiments in particular. We tried to anticipate and defend against them in the following ways.

In the first place, to minimize the artificial and perhaps reactive nature of our research setting, we made certain that our experimental manipulations were as unobtrusive as possible. The cutting, splicing, and rearranging of news stories were accomplished with state-of-the-art editing equipment that left behind no telltale traces. Even the most dedicated television news afficionado would have been hard pressed to detect any of the changes we introduced. We also encouraged participants to watch the news in a relaxed manner, and provided them with coffee, newspapers, and magazines. Many participants came with friends, spouses, or other family members. As we had intended, the sessions took on a casual atmosphere, with participants chatting among themselves, glancing around the room, browsing through the newspapers and magazines, and occasionally hooting at the commercials.

Second, because we were interested in assessing the impact of television news on ordinary Americans, not on college sophomores, we generally avoided that most convenient of populations.[2] Instead, by circulating advertisements widely in two quite different communities (New Haven, Connecticut and Ann Arbor, Michigan), we had hoped to lure a wide cross-section of people into our experiments.

In this respect, our experiments were highly successful. Table 2.1 presents a demographic and political profile of sequential experimental participants; table 2.2 does the same for assemblage experiments. As revealed in the two tables, participants in our experiments did indeed come in all varieties: young and old; black and white; men and women; poorly educated and well-educated; blue collar workers and professionals; Democrats, Independents, and Republicans; devoted to and oblivious of television news. Moreover, in aggregate terms, the profiles drawn in tables 2.1 and 2.2 are quite faithful to national figures. It would of course be absurd to pretend that participants in our experiments constitute a representative sample of the national population— or of any population, for that matter. They do not. Nevertheless, it is fair to say that the experimental results presented in the chapters ahead are based upon the reactions of a diverse group of ordinary Americans.

Third, none of our conclusions or interpretations depends upon a single (and perhaps peculiar) comparison. As a general rule, we have followed a strategy of conceptual replication: repeated tests with conceptually identical but empirically different realizations of the variables under investigation. Thus the same hypothesis was tested with different national problems and with different news stories. Similarly, we assessed participants' political opinions in a variety of ways. Within each experiment, we sometimes invited participants to define problems in their own terms; at other times they were taken through a battery of questions with built-in response alternatives. Where possible, we made use of questions that had undergone extensive testing and development by the Center for Political Studies, as part of the periodic National Election Studies. These procedures provide some assurance that any particular result is not specific to a particular problem, to a particular newscast, or to the particular questions we put to our participants.

TABLE 2.1

Demographic and Political Profile of Sequential Experiment Participants

Age		*Occupation**	
Range	19–68	Blue collar	41%
Average	31	Service/clerical	35
Race		Managerial/professional	24
White	82%	*Party Identification*	
Nonwhite	18	Democrat	39%
Sex		Independent	35
Male	48%	Republican	12
Female	52	Other/no preference	14
Education		*TV News Viewing*	
High school or less	35%	Never/hardly ever	23%
Some college	29	Two-three/week	48
College graduate	36	Every evening	29

Note: Number of participants = 259.

*Among those with full-time employment

TABLE 2.2

Demographic and Political Profile of Assemblage Experiment Participants

Age		*Occupation**	
Range	18–81	Blue collar	26%
Average	33	Service/clerical	46
Race		Managerial/professional	28
White	82%	*Party Identification*	
Nonwhite	18	Democrat	39%
Sex		Independent	35
Male	51%	Republican	10
Female	49	Other/no preference	15
Education		*TV News Viewing*	
High school or less	34%	Never/hardly ever	23%
Some college	31	Two-three/week	40
College graduate	35	Every evening	37

Note: Number of participants = 772. The table excludes two assemblage experiments (3 and 11), because they were based on college undergraduates.

*Among those with full-time employment

By diminishing the artificiality of the experimental setting, drawing upon heterogenous groups of experimental participants, and following a strategy of conceptual replication, we have reduced the hazards of generalizing from our experimental results. However, the scandal of induction is still with us. The risks of generalizing from experiments can never be entirely eliminated.

Fortunately, the limitations of experimentation correspond to strengths in other methodological approaches. Although the results we report in the chapters ahead come predominantly from experiments, they are supplemented at several critical junctures by results from our own analysis of national surveys. In this we are trying to practice the methodological pluralism the late Carl Hovland (1959) was urging a quarter century ago. By examining television news from several methodological angles, we escape the limitations inherent in any single approach. We emphasize and promote experiments because of their real advantages and because for the most part media specialists have so assiduously ignored them. But we are methodological pluralists at heart.

The Agenda-Setting Effect

In *The Phantom Public,* Walter Lippmann characterized the political sensibilities of the ordinary American this way:

The private citizen today has come to feel rather like a deaf spectator in the back row, who ought to keep his mind on the mystery off there, but cannot quite manage to keep awake. He knows he is somehow affected by what is going on. Rules and regulations continually, taxes annually and wars occasionally remind him that he is being swept along by great drifts of circumstance.

Yet these public affairs are in no convincing way his affairs. They are for the most part invisible. They are managed, if they are managed at all, at distant centers, from behind the scenes, by unnamed powers. As a private person he does not know for certain what is going on, or who is doing it, or where he is being carried (1925, 13).

From this perspective, that ordinary citizens achieve any understanding of public affairs seems rather remarkable. Moreover, the "swarming confusion of problems" that, according to Lippmann, constituted political life more than a half century ago, has grown only more confusing today. Surely the democratic predicament of the ordinary citizen has deepened.

Television news may provide citizens with a convenient escape from this predicament. In this chapter we being to investigate how, if at all, television news influences Americans' conceptions of political reality— their sense of "the mystery off there." Our point of departure is the *agenda-setting hypothesis: those problems that receive prominent attention on the national news become the problems the viewing public regards as the nation's most important.* We pursue this hypothesis with sequential experiments, assemblage experiments, and a longitudinal analysis of national surveys.

Experimental Tests of Agenda-Setting

SEQUENTIAL EXPERIMENTS

Four sequential experiments provide evidence relevant to the agenda-setting hypothesis. Each systematically varied the amount of coverage that the evening news devoted to various national problems. Experiment 1 is the prototype; we will therefore describe it in detail and then move expeditiously through the rest. (Detailed summaries of all fourteen experiments are presented in Appendix A.)

Experiment 1 was conducted in New Haven, Connecticut during six consecutive days in November of 1980, shortly after the presidential election. Participants watched recordings of the previous evening's network newscasts that had been edited in advance, as described in chapter 2. The thirteen participants randomly assigned to the *treatment condition* in experiment 1 were shown stories that described inadequacies in American defense preparedness. The first edited broadcast included a report on the increase in defense spending to be proposed by the incoming Reagan administration. The next day's newscast featured a "special assignment" report on the declining role of the U.S. as the arsenal of democracy. Spliced into the third day's broadcast was a pessimistic analysis of U.S. military options in the event of Soviet aggression in the Persian Gulf. And the fourth day's broadcast included a story that set out the considerable difficulty the U.S. Army was encountering in finding recruits qualified to operate its increasingly sophisticated equipment. Over the four days, then, participants in the treatment condition saw four stories on defense, totaling seventeen minutes of news coverage. The fifteen participants randomly assigned to the *control condition,* in contrast, watched broadcasts containing no defense-related stories at all.[1]

In experiment 1, as in all those that follow, participants were, of course, *randomly* assigned to conditions. According to information gathered on the first day of experiment 1, this procedure had the intended result: that is, participants assigned to the defense condition did not differ from their counterparts assigned to the control condition. On demographic characteristics, partisanship, and political engagement, the two groups were indistinguishable.[2] This means that whatever postexperimental differences between groups we detect can confidently be attributed to differences in the newscasts they watched.

In order to test the agenda-setting hypothesis, we measured participants' beliefs about the importance of national problems both before and after the experimental sessions. The preexperimental questionnaire was administered immediately before the first newscast and the postexperimental questionnaire was completed one full day after the last newscast. On both occasions, participants judged the importance of each of eight national problems, indicated their personal concern for each, the extent to which each was deserving of additional government action, and the frequency with which they talked about each in everyday conversation.[3] Because these four ratings were strongly intercorrelated, they were averaged together to form a composite index of problem importance. A score of zero on the index means that the participant thought the problem not important at all; cared not at all about it; felt that people in government should worry about it not at all; and that the problem never served as a topic of conversation. A score of one hundred means, in contrast, that the participant thought the problem extremely important; cared about it very much; felt that the government should worry about it a lot; and talked about it almost incessantly. Of course, virtually all participants rated the problems somewhere between these two extremes.[4]

The critical test of agenda-setting simply entails observation of change over the experiment in the importance participants accord the problems emphasized by the edited newscasts. In experiment 1, participants who viewed newscasts that described glaring inadequacies in U.S. defense capabilities should become more concerned about defense than control condition participants whose newscasts were purged of such stories.

This is exactly what happened. Participants in the defense condition became more concerned about defense over the experiment's six days, while participants in the control condition showed no change in the importance they attached to defense. This difference is significant both statistically and politically.[5] Consider the evidence in detail: on the first day of experiment 1, *before* seeing any newscasts, participants who were randomly assigned to the defense treatment condition ranked defense sixth in relative importance, behind inflation, pollution, unemployment, energy, and civil rights. *After* exposure to the newscasts, the same participants now believed that defense was the country's second most important problem, trailing only inflation. Among viewers in the control condition, meanwhile, the relative position of defense as a national problem did not change.

Such a dramatic shift in priorities, induced by such a modest and unobtrusive alteration in television news coverage, constitutes powerful confirmation of the agenda-setting hypothesis. Moreover, what we found in experiment 1 we found again and again in three additional sequential experiments.

Experiment 2 took place in late February 1981 and focused on three problems. Depending on condition, participants viewed newscasts that emphasized either inadequacies in U.S. defense preparedness, pollution of the environment, or soaring inflation. Experiment 8, administered in July 1982, featured newscasts that concentrated either on unemployment, nuclear arms control, or civil rights. And in experiment 9, which took place in August 1982, participants either viewed a sequence of newscasts that emphasized unemployment or saw no newscasts at all. In other respects, each of these three sequential experiments followed experiment 1's basic design. The recruitment of participants, the splicing in and editing out of stories, the questionnaires administered on the first day and on the sixth: all these procedures were followed as described previously. Counting experiment 1, then, we have eight separate and independent tests of agenda-setting, distributed across four experiments and six different problems.

The results from all four sequential experiments are displayed together in table 3.1. The table shows the average composite importance rating of the target problem before and after exposure to the newscasts. The message could not be clearer. In *every* instance, participants emerged from our experiments believing that the target problem was more important than they did when they began. Seven of the eight changes are statistically significant.

The single exception to this pattern, which occurred in the inflation condition of experiment 2, is no great mystery. In February of 1981, when experiment 2 took place, inflation was running at an annual rate of more than 10 percent. In the preexperimental questionnaire, before they glimpsed a single inflation news story, participants gave inflation an average score of ninety-two on our composite scale of zero to one hundred. Thus we had virtually no opportunity to convince participants of inflation's importance: everyone was already convinced.

Putting this exception aside, the four sequential experiments yield striking evidence of agenda-setting. As in experiment 1, the changes observed in experiments 2, 8, and 9 correspond to substantial shifts in

TABLE 3.1

Change in Problem Importance

		Importance Rating of Problem		
Experiment	Problem	Before the Experiment	After the Experiment	Change: Pre- to Post-
1	Defense	47	67	20*
2	Defense	48	58	10*
	Inflation	92	93	01
	Pollution	63	76	13*
8	Arms control	76	82	06*
	Civil rights	64	69	05*
	Unemployment	75	82	07*
9	Unemployment	78	83	05*

*$p < .05$

problem hierarchies. In experiment 2, for example, pollution as a national problem moved up from fifth to second most important among participants shown news about pollution, while defense rose from sixth to fourth among participants who watched newscasts that emphasized U.S. defense weaknesses. Similar shifts occurred in the relative importance of arms control, civil rights, and unemployment in experiments 8 and 9.

The agenda-setting hypothesis can be tested in a second way. In experiments 2, 8, and 9 (though regrettably not in 1), the questionnaire asked participants to name "the three most important problems facing the nation." As a second test, therefore, we can compare the proportion that mentioned the target problem in the preexperimental questionnaire with the proportion naming it in the postexperimental questionnaire, following exposure to the altered newscasts. These comparisons are shown in table 3.2.

As indicated there, the evidence in support of agenda-setting is even more striking for this measure than it was for composite ratings. Except, once again, for the inflation condition in experiment 2—where *every* participant named inflation as one of the country's most important problems, both before and after the experiment—references to the target problem were more numerous after the newscasts than before. Some of these increases are massive. In experiment 8, for example, after exposure to coverage of the perils of the arms race, the percentage of participants naming arms control as one of the country's three most important problems rose from 35 percent to 65 percent; in experiment 9, the corresponding percentage, this time for unemployment, increased from 50 percent to 86 percent. Over the seven inde-

TABLE 3.2

Change in Problem Importance

		Percentage Naming Problem as One of Country's Most Serious		
Experiment	Problem	Before the Experiment	After the Experiment	Change: Pre- to Post-
2	Defense	33	53	20*
	Inflation	100	100	00
	Pollution	0	14	14*
8	Arms control	35	65	30*
	Civil rights	0	10	10*
	Unemployment	43	71	28*
9	Unemployment	50	86	36*

*$p < .05$

pendent tests, an average of 37 percent nominated the target problem as one of the nation's most important in the preexperimental questionnaire; 57 percent did so in the postexperimental questionnaire.[6]

We also assessed the *specificity* of these effects. In general, we looked for "spillover" in agenda-setting. We supposed that drawing viewers' attention to a particular problem might enhance not only the importance they ascribe to that problem but to related problems as well. For example, stories emphasizing dependence on foreign sources of oil might reasonably be expected to raise concern about rising prices, since the public seems to regard the two problems as causally linked (Hendricks and Denney 1979). Reasonable or not, we encountered such spillover effects in only two instances. In experiment 8, participants exposed to news about the arms race became more concerned not only with arms control but also with the conflict in the Middle East. In experiment 9, participants furnished with coverage of unemployment became more concerned about economic problems in general. As a rule, however, the agenda-setting effects we uncovered are notable for their specificity. News about energy influenced viewers' beliefs about the importance of energy and energy alone; news about defense influenced viewers' beliefs about defense and defense alone; and so on.

In sum, the evidence from the four sequential experiments strongly supports the agenda-setting hypothesis. With a single and understandable exception, problems given steady news coverage grow more important, at least in the minds of the viewers. The evening news would seem to possess a powerful capacity to shape the public's national priorities.

ASSEMBLAGE EXPERIMENTS

In sequential experiments viewers are exposed either to a sustained dose of news about a particular problem or to no news at all. One virtue of assemblage experiments is that they permit a more precise calibration of treatment conditions. Here we examine six such experiments in an effort to learn more about the functional relationship between the amount of news coverage and the size of the agenda-setting effect.

Experiment 3 was conducted in New Haven during April and May of 1981 with Yale University undergraduates. Students viewed a forty-minute collection of "typical" news stories that paid either no attention to the nation's energy problems (zero stories), some attention (three stories) or considerable attention (six stories).

Experiment 4 was run in New Haven during late September to early

October 1981. This time participants were recruited from the general community and randomly assigned to one of six experimental treatments. Participants watched a collection of fifteen news stories that gave either moderate attention (three stories) or extensive attention (six stories) to one of three national problems: defense, energy, or inflation. Participants assigned to either the moderate or extensive treatment conditions for any one problem (say defense) saw *no* stories about the other two (energy, inflation). This design enables us to assess the agenda-setting effect induced by some exposure to a problem versus none, as well as the impact induced by incremental increases in coverage.

Experiment 5, which took place in New Haven during August–September of 1981, followed this same design, with two amendments. First, in place of stories about defense, energy, and inflation, we substituted stories about unemployment, civil rights, and social security. Second, we reduced the number of stories bearing on the target problem in the moderate and extensive coverage conditions to two and four, respectively.

Experiments 6, 13, and 14 represent the natural culmination of this trend of diminishing experimental interventions. In experiment 6, conducted in New Haven in May and June of 1981, participants watched a collection of news stories that included either just a *single* story about the target problem—this time either pollution or unemployment—or no stories at all. Likewise, in experiment 13, run in Ann Arbor in June 1983, and in experiment 14, conducted in New Haven in August of 1983: in the former instance, participants watched a collection that included one story either about unemployment or energy; in the latter, participants were exposed to a collection that featured a single story either about government efforts to halt drug smuggling or about the difficulties facing public schools.[7]

We measured problem importance in these six assemblage experiments just as we did in the sequential experiments: i.e., by composite ratings and spontaneous mentions.[8] The test of agenda-setting is different here, though, because assemblage designs forego the preexperimental questionnaire that is a standard fixture of the sequential design. Participants in assemblage experiments complete only one questionnaire, immediately following exposure to the news presentations. Therefore, the appropriate test of agenda-setting here is to compare the importance participants attach to a target problem across different experimental conditions representing different levels of coverage.

The results for the composite importance ratings are shown in table

3.3. The rows reflect different problems across the six experiments; the columns reflect intensity of coverage, from no news stories at all on the left to a maximum of six stories on the right. If the agenda-setting hypothesis holds, the importance ratings of the various target problems should increase from left to right as coverage intensifies—and they generally do. In fact, twelve of the thirteen ratings increase, ten to a statistically significantly degree. As was true in sequential experiments, agenda-setting proved elusive only for those problems that were regarded as highly important at the outset. In the case of inflation in experiment 4, for example, a virtual bombardment of coverage—six stories in a collection of fifteen—was required to boost ratings still higher than those offered by viewers who saw no stories about inflation.

Support for agenda-setting is generally more striking when importance is measured by the spontaneous nomination of national problems, shown in table 3.4. In every instance but one, participants shown some stories about a particular problem—as many as six stories or as

TABLE 3.3

Problem Importance as a Function of Intensity of Coverage

Experiment	Problem	Composite Ratings							
		Number of Stories							Difference: Maximum Coverage Minus No Coverage
		0	1	2	3	4	5	6	
3	Energy	64			66			74	10***
4	Defense	58			63			70	12***
	Energy	72			67			72	00
	Inflation	81			81			90	09***
5	Civil rights	69		71		86			17***
	Social security	77		84		88			11***
	Unemployment	78		87		84			06*
6	Pollution	77	81						04***
	Unemployment	88	89						01
13	Unemployment	90	95						05***
	Energy	75	68						−07
14	Drugs	43	53						10***
	Education	70	74						04*

  *$p < .20$
 **$p < .10$
***$p < .05$

TABLE 3.4

Problem Importance as a Function of Intensity of Coverage

Experiment	Problem	Percentage Naming Problem as One of Country's Most Serious							Difference: Maximum Coverage Minus No Coverage
		Number of Stories							
		0	1	2	3	4	5	6	
3	Energy	24			50			65	41***
4	Defense	33			57			64	31***
	Energy	21			46			46	25***
	Inflation	45			50			79	34***
5	Civil rights	15		29		33			18**
	Social security	10		41		44			34***
	Unemployment	30		30		67			37***
6	Pollution	10	27						17***
	Unemployment	53	73						20***
13	Unemployment	50	68						18**
	Energy	0	23						23
14	Drugs	0	11						11***
	Education	14	11						−03

 *$p < .20$
 **$p < .10$
 ***$p < .05$

few as one—were more likely to name that problem as one of the country's most important than were those whose attention was directed elsewhere. All but one of these differences surpass statistical significance and some of them are extraordinary.[9] In experiment 5, for example, whereas less than one-third of the participants exposed to two stories on unemployment named it as one of the country's most serious problems, fully two-thirds of those exposed to four stories on unemployment did so. Perhaps the most arresting result of all is that agenda-setting can be triggered by such ostensibly innocuous provocations. In experiments 6, 13, and 14, viewers' priorities were significantly affected by a *single* news story.

PERSISTENCE OF AGENDA-SETTING

Measurable immediate influence is not the same as influence that lasts, of course. We assessed the influence of television news in assemblage experiments immediately following the broadcasts. Sequential experiments are somewhat more informative, but they tell us only that television news's influence is detectable twenty-four hours after the experimental intervention is completed. That the effects survive this long is certainly important. Television dispenses news periodically, typically on cycles of twenty-four hours or less. The regularity and frequency of broadcasts means that for many viewers, agenda-setting is a continuous process. When the networks develop priorities, viewers' beliefs are affected—and affected again as new priorities arise. Having said that, however, we are still left with the question of how long our experimentally-induced effects last.

We designed experiments 13 and 14 partly to investigate the persistence of agenda-setting effects. In the former, we reinterviewed as many participants as possible over the telephone one week after they had been exposed to our news broadcast. Participants were told that we were conducting an opinion poll of the Ann Arbor community. Virtually everyone we were able to reach agreed to participate (75 percent of the original group). In the followup to experiment 14, we mailed to each participant a second questionnaire one week after their experimental session. Eighty-three of the original 121 participants (69 percent) completed and returned the questionnaire. In both followup sessions, among many other questions, participants were asked to name the country's most serious problems. Experiments 13 and 14 thereby afford a test of the persistence of agenda-setting effects—and a stringent one at that. The two experiments are not only assemblage designs, which produce less powerful effects than do sequential designs, but they represent the weakest of the assemblage designs, involving as they do only a single story.[10]

Nevertheless, both experiments reveal evidence of persistence. These results are displayed in table 3.5. As indicated there, participants in experiment 13 who had been exposed to a single story about unemployment continued, one week later, to nominate unemployment more frequently as one of the country's most important problems than did those who saw no news about unemployment. This difference was virtually as great at one week's remove from the experimental intervention as it was immediately afterwards. More generally, the table shows that the agenda-setting effect was maintained over the one week period in two instances, diminished in one, and actually strengthened in another. Keeping in mind that alterations in viewers' political priorities were prompted originally by a single story, the degree of persistence revealed here is remarkable.

TABLE 3.5

Immediate and Delayed Effects of Coverage on Problem Importance

		Percentage Naming Problem as One of Country's Most Serious					
		Immediate:			One Week Later:		
		Number of Stories			Number of Stories		
Experi- ment	Problem	0	1	Difference	0	1	Difference
13	Unemployment	46	72	+26**	54	73	+19**
	Energy	0	15	+15	4	8	+ 4
14	Drugs	0	14	+14***	0	14	+14***
	Education	14	13	− 1	8	26	+18***

Note: Table includes only those participants interviewed immediately after the experiment *and* one week later.

  $*p < .20$
 $**p < .10$
$***p < .05$

Time Series Tests of Agenda-Setting [11]

Our experimental results suggest that television newscasts shape and intensify viewers' sense of which national problems are important and which are not. But do our experimental results generalize to the natural setting that is our real interest? We think they do—partly because of the convergence of findings across experiments, problems, and populations; partly because of the steps we took to diminish the artificiality of our experiments—but we cannot be completely confident.

To bolster our confidence and complement our experimental results, we undertook a nonexperimental test of agenda-setting. We examined trends in television news coverage over time, and compared them with changes over comparable periods in public opinion. Prior efforts of this sort suggest that there should be a correspondence between the two, and a strong one. Thus Funkhouser (1973) discovered striking concurrence between the amount and timing of attention paid to various problems in the national press between 1960 and 1970 and the importance accorded those problems by the American public. Across the decade, public opinion seemed to follow, not lead, the press's agenda, results that were substantially fortified by the more sophisticated analyses that followed (MacKuen 1981, 1984).

Funkhouser and MacKuen presumed, as we do, that agenda-setting effects should be observed and estimated over time, as problems appear and disappear, and as network news coverage shifts accordingly. What we have attempted to do in our experiments is convert the variation in coverage that occurs naturally over time to contemporaneous variation across experimental conditions. We create and then offer to our viewers alternative portrayals of political reality. As an important check on the experimental results, here we will determine through time-series analysis the extent to which the preoccupations of network news become the political preoccupations of the American public.

For this purpose, we compiled results from national surveys between 1974 to 1980 pertaining to three prominent national problems: energy, inflation, and unemployment. By ransacking Gallup, Yankelovich, and Center for Political Studies surveys, we were able to obtain a measure of the importance attached by the public to each of the three problems for every two-month period between January 1974 and December 1980.[12] Our specific measure of problem importance stems from "the most important problem facing the nation." Unfortunately, the exact wording, format, and coding of the question varies across survey organizations. Gallup and Yankelovich accept multiple answers while CPS does not; and Yankelovich interviewers consistently "pull" more answers from survey respondents than do Gallup's. To ensure comparability in results across the three survey organizations, we took as our dependent variable the percentage of *responses* to the question rather than the percentage of *respondents*. (For a detailed explanation of this procedure, see Appendix B).

We measured television news coverage of the three problems by recording the number of pertinent news stories appearing in the weekday CBS Evening News.[13] Using the Vanderbilt Television Archive's *Abstracts* of daily newscasts as our source, we classified news stories on the basis of their major focus (news stories that lasted less than thirty seconds were excluded). The number of news stories for each problem was totaled for every month and then averaged for each bimonthly observation.

Measured in this way, the attention provided these three problems by television news underwent dramatic changes between 1974 and 1980. Figure 3.1 displays the 1974–80 time graphs for energy; figure 3.2 does so for inflation; figure 3.3 provides the same information for unemployment. Between 1974 and 1980, CBS's coverage of energy ranged from two stories per month to fifty-eight stories per month. Inflation received as few as six stories per month to as many as thirty-seven. Monthly coverage of unemployment ranged between no stories at all to a modest peak of seven.

Over the same period there were also striking changes in the importance the American public ascribed to the three problems. The proportion of the public naming energy as one of the country's most important problems fluctuated from a low of 2 percent to a high of 34 percent; inflation, from 19 to 72 percent; and unemployment, from 2 to 32 percent (see figures 3.1, 3.2, and 3.3). And to the naked eye, at least, these fluctuations in public concern seem to move roughly in tandem with fluctuations in television news coverage.

That the trends move together does not, of course, tell us anything about the *causal* impact of television news coverage on problem importance. The parallel trends might mean that news coverage influences public opinion, but it could mean just the reverse: that news organizations respond to the public's priorities. In order to attract the largest audience, the networks might feature stories about inflation when the public seems concerned about inflation and stories about unemployment when the public seems preoccupied by unemployment. Or the correspondence in the over-time trends might reflect that the networks and the public are responding in concert to real changes in the world. Soaring prices are noticed in New York as in Peoria, with implications that are easy to imagine for both the networks and the public. Our task

FIGURE 3.1

TV News Coverage and Public Opinion toward Energy, 1974–1980

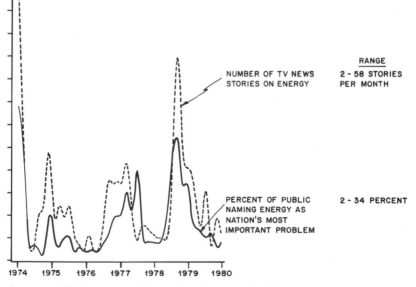

Source: AIPO, Yankelovich, National Election Studies Surveys; Vanderbilt TV News Abstracts

must be to determine not just the association between television news and public opinion, but rather the precise causal impact (if any) of television news on public opinion.

To do so, we relied on a procedure that computes a consistent estimate of the impact of television news coverage on public opinion purged of the reverse effect, if any, of public opinion on news coverage (see Appendix B for the technical details). This procedure also estimates the impact of television coverage over and above the effects due to real world conditions. Because energy shortages, price increases, and job loss can all be experienced personally, they may influence public opinion directly. To take such effects into account, we coded various measures of real world conditions and incorporated them into our analysis. They included the cost and availability of energy, American dependence on foreign sources of energy, meetings of OPEC oil ministers in the energy analysis; various aggregate indicators of prices and interest rates in the inflation analysis; and aggregate measures of the extent of unemployment and change in unemployment in the unemployment analysis. Finally, we also included a measure of major presidential speeches devoted primarily to energy, inflation, or unemployment (see

FIGURE 3.2

TV News Coverage and Public Opinion toward Inflation, 1974–1980

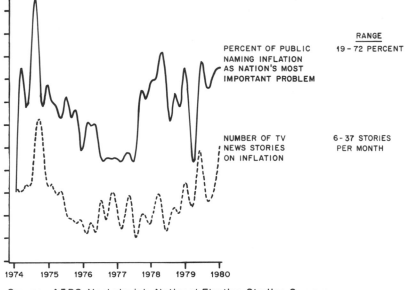

RANGE
19 – 72 PERCENT

PERCENT OF PUBLIC
NAMING INFLATION
AS NATION'S MOST
IMPORTANT PROBLEM

NUMBER OF TV
NEWS STORIES
ON INFLATION

6 – 37 STORIES
PER MONTH

1974   1975   1976   1977   1978   1979   1980

Source: AIPO, Yankelovich, National Election Studies Surveys;
    Vanderbilt TV News Abstracts

Appendix B for details on all these measures). In short, our analysis attempts to reveal the degree to which television news influences public opinion, independent of the effects due to actual conditions and to presidential efforts to mobilize public opinion.

The results for energy are shown in table 3.6.[14] As indicated there, television news coverage does indeed influence the importance the American public attaches to energy. For every seven stories broadcast, public responses citing energy as one of the country's most important problems increased by about 1 percent. Notice that this is a *contemporaneous* effect: television coverage in the current period influences public opinion in the current period. We also tested for but could not find lagged effects: i.e., the amount of coverage devoted to energy during any two-month period apparently had no effect on opinion toward energy expressed during the next two-month period. Perhaps surprisingly, public opinion on energy was unaffected by real world conditions. Energy costs, fuel oil costs in particular, dependence on OPEC imports, OPEC oil minister meetings: none of these boosted public concern with energy independently of television news coverage.[15] The public's concern for energy *was* shaped independently by the presi-

FIGURE 3.3

TV News Coverage and Public Opinion toward Unemployment, 1974–1980

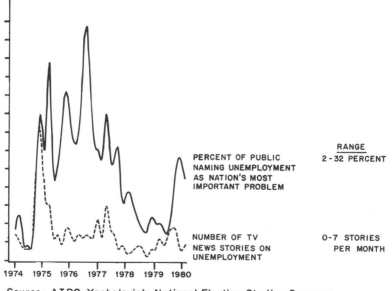

PERCENT OF PUBLIC
NAMING UNEMPLOYMENT
AS NATION'S MOST
IMPORTANT PROBLEM

RANGE
2 - 32 PERCENT

NUMBER OF TV
NEWS STORIES ON
UNEMPLOYMENT

0-7 STORIES
PER MONTH

1974   1975   1976   1977   1978   1979   1980

Source: AIPO, Yankelovich, National Election Studies Surveys;
         Vanderbilt TV News Abstracts

TABLE 3.6

Predictors of Public Opinion toward Energy, January 1974–December 1980
(Two-stage, maximum likelihood estimates)

Predictors	Coefficient
Number of stories on energy	.13*
Presidential speeches on energy	4.44*
Constant	12.52*
Adjusted R^2 = .55	
Standard error of regression = 3.20	
Durbin-Watson statistic = 2.06	

Number of observations = 42.

*$p < .05$

dent, however. When the president chose to address the nation on the subject of energy, he succeeded in raising the level of public concern by over 4 percent.

The American public's preoccupation with inflation between 1974 and 1980 was determined by a similar combination of news coverage and presidential rhetoric (see table 3.7). The number of television news stories about inflation significantly increased the percent of responses naming inflation as the nation's most important problem. On average, five stories per month on inflation elevated public concern by 1 percent (again, an entirely contemporaneous effect), whereas a presidential address to the nation on the economy increased the degree of public concern about inflation by over 8 percent. Again, actual conditions had no direct impact on public opinion: changes in the consumer price index, the consumer price index for food, and interest rates were

TABLE 3.7

Predictors of Public Opinion toward Inflation, January 1974–December 1980
(Ordinary least square estimates)

Predictors	Coefficient
Number of news stories on inflation	.21*
Presidential speeches on inflation	8.26*
Constant	41.92*
Adjusted R^2 = .49	
Standard error of regression = 7.38	
Durbin-Watson statistic = 1.54	

Number of observations = 42.

*$p < .05$

all unrelated to the importance the American public attached to inflation, once the influence of television news coverage was taken into
account.[16]

This brings us finally to the case of unemployment, where television
news effects appear to be weaker. As shown in table 3.8, eleven stories
per month were required to boost public concern about unemployment by a single percentage point. Moreover, on statistical grounds,
we cannot be certain that television news coverage had *any* effect at
all. And unlike public opinion on energy and inflation, the American
public's concern about unemployment was unaffected by presidential
addresses. Instead, the importance of unemployment to the American
public was determined by actual conditions. As unemployment spread
and deepened, more and more Americans considered it to be among
the country's most pressing problems, largely independently of trends
in television news coverage.

The comparatively frail results uncovered for television's impact
on public concern about unemployment may be due to the chronically
low level of news coverage. Over the seven-year period under examination here (which preceded the dramatic increases in unemployment
that occurred in 1981 and 1982), CBS broadcast an average of just four
stories on unemployment every two months. This represents less than
one-third of the coverage CBS gave to energy and less than one-fourth
of the attention the network devoted to inflation. If the *networks* regard unemployment as less newsworthy than rising prices or energy
shortages, then so, too, may the public.

This point aside, we should not be deflected from the central message carried by the time-series results. Here we find strong convergent

TABLE 3.8

Predictors of Public Opinion toward Unemployment, January 1974–December 1980
(Maximum likelihood estimates)

Predictors	Coefficient
Number of news stories on unemployment	.09
Unemployment rate	3.18*
Average duration of unemployment (weeks)	1.41*
Constant	−23.34*
Adjusted R^2 = .50	
Standard error of regression = 3.98	
Durbin-Watson statistic = 1.89	

Number of observations = 42.
*$p < .05$

support for television agenda-setting. Between 1974 and 1980, the American public's political preoccupations underwent sharp changes, changes that we have traced in part to changing patterns of television news coverage.[17]

CONCLUSION

Taken all together, our evidence decisively sustains the agenda-setting hypothesis. The verdict is clear and unequivocal: It issues from sequential experiments that last a week, from assemblage experiments that last an hour, and from time-series data that span seven years; it holds across different measures of importance; and it is confirmed for a variety of problems, from national defense to social security. By attending to some problems and ignoring others, television news shapes the American public's political priorities. These effects appear to be neither momentary, as our experimental results indicate, nor permanent, as our time-series results reveal.

All told our evidence implies an American public with a limited memory for last month's news and a recurrent vulnerability to today's. When television news focuses on a problem, the public's priorities are altered, and altered again as television news moves on to something new.

Vivid Cases and Lead Stories

The death of a single Russian soldier is a tragedy. A million deaths is a statistic.

Josef Stalin[1]

You can't turn on the evening news without seeing that they're going to interview someone else who has lost his job. Is it news that some fellow out in South Succotash someplace has just been laid off and that he should be interviewed nationwide?

Ronald Reagan[2]

Thus far we have limited our analysis of agenda-setting to the sheer quantity of coverage that network news devotes to national problems. But surely viewers are influenced not only by the amount of news but also by the *kind* of news they see. How television news frames a problem may be as important as whether the problem appears on the air at all. In this chapter we investigate two such possibilities: first, whether agenda-setting is enhanced by stories that illustrate and personalize national problems (the vividness hypothesis); and second, whether stories that appear at the top of the broadcast are more influential in setting the public's agenda than stories that appear later in the newscast (the lead story hypothesis).

THE VIVIDNESS HYPOTHESIS

On April 21, 1982, CBS presented "People Like Us," an hour-long examination of cutbacks in government services implemented by the Reagan administration. Narrated by Bill Moyers, the documentary focused on four Americans: an Ohio man with cerebral palsy who had lost his disability benefits, a New Jersey Hispanic woman forced to quit her job and go back on welfare so that her ailing son would be eligible for government benefits, a 13-year-old comatose Wisconsin girl taken out of her home and placed in an institution, and a Milwaukee priest, who distributed food to the poor. "People Like Us" drew attention to

34

Americans who had somehow, in the rhetoric of the day, fallen through President Reagan's safety net. It concluded with these words from Moyers: "The burden falls most heavily on the poor, and some of the truly needy are truly hurting . . . For all the fraud and waste, for all their inefficiencies, these programs are a life-support system for the poor. For many, we are pulling the plug."

White House reaction was swift and strong. David Gergen, White House communications director, angrily denounced the documentary, arguing that it unfairly blamed President Reagan for poverty and hunger, and petitioned CBS for time to reply (CBS declined). The administration was obviously deeply concerned that "People Like Us" had made its point effectively. Vivid sketches of individual Americans struggling valiantly to hold body and soul together seemed a searing indictment of the President's policies.

This episode is but one illustration of a pervasive assumption. Politicians, journalists, and social scientists alike point to the special power allegedly inherent in presenting news through pictures. Under this assumption, it is one thing to read accounts of civil rights protests; quite another to see film of police attack dogs set loose on black protestors. It is one thing to understand that American boys are fighting and dying in Vietnam; quite another to watch them fight and die. In each case, so it is argued, the concrete visual details matter enormously.

In their influential summary of research on the shortcomings and strengths of everyday judgment, the psychologists Nisbett and Ross agree. They argue that people are often persuaded by information that is distinguished primarily by its perceptual prominence. In so doing, they become victims of a vividness bias, giving "inferential weight to information in proportion to its vividness" (1980, 62). Nisbett and Ross lament this tendency—it is a shortcoming, not a strength of judgment—since vivid information is not necessarily relevant or even informative.

Nisbett and Ross's claim appears straightforward enough, and it is certainly intuitively compelling. But the evidence is not. The relevant literature is littered with weak and even negative results, and, predictably enough, with disagreements over the very meaning of vividness. There is one clear instance of the vividness bias, however. When vividness is defined as the contrast between personalized, case history information and abstract statistical information, the vividness hypothesis is supported every time. In one such experiment, for example, participants' beliefs about the character and motivation of welfare recipients were influenced much more by a vivid depiction of a single welfare recipient than they were by a report summarizing in statistical form the characteristics of all welfare recipients (Hamill, Wilson, and Nisbett 1980). In other experiments, too, vivid but questionably informative case histories overpower highly informative but dull statistics (Taylor and Thompson 1982).

It is vividness defined in just these terms that is of particular interest here. As in "People Like Us," television news often provides close glimpses of particular victims in order to illustrate national problems, dramatic vignettes that bring home the personal ramifications of the great public issues of the day. A network news story on recession, for example, may be followed up by a piercing interview with an unemployed auto worker longing for work, angry, afraid, slipping into alcoholism and depression. Reuven Frank, former president of NBC's news division, argues that television news does this, and *should* do it, because "the highest power of television journalism is not in the transmission of information but in the transmission of experience" (quoted in Epstein 1973, 242). Our interest here lies not with the desirability of this practice but with its effectiveness. Do vivid case studies strengthen the ability of the networks to shape the American public's political priorities?

EXPERIMENTAL TESTS OF THE VIVIDNESS HYPOTHESIS

We designed experiments 6 and 11 to assess the power of vivid news presentations. Participants in experiment 6 were residents of the New Haven area, recruited in the usual manner during November and December of 1981. All were shown a videotape comprised of nine stories previously broadcast on the networks' evening news. The key treatment story focused either on environmental hazards or on unemployment and appeared midway through the broadcast in all experimental conditions. Participants assigned to one of the four environmental hazards conditions watched a story about either toxic waste in Massachusetts or asbestos contamination in Arizona, presented either in vivid or pallid versions. With regard to unemployment, participants saw a story about either high levels of joblessness in Chicago or forthcoming cuts in the Comprehensive Employment Training Act (CETA) presented, again, either in vivid or pallid versions.

We define *vivid* information by its attention to personalized case histories. Vivid news in experiment 6 focuses on specific victims of environmental hazards or unemployment, while *pallid* news deals in abstract concepts or general trends. For example, one of the target stories covered the apparent connection between a toxic waste disposal site and the high incidence of childhood leukemia in a Massachusetts community. In the vivid format, after a stormy interview with the mother of one of the stricken children, her son looks innocently into the camera and expresses the hope, obviously faint, that he will soon be able to play with his friends. In the pallid version, a reporter merely discusses the possible link between the chemical dump and catastrophic illness, and traces the political controversy it has produced. In the vivid version of the hard times in Chicago story, to take a second example, viewers saw an earnest young black man attempting unsuccessfully to find work. During the story he is seen with his troubled family and they describe the various hardships caused by unemployment. In the pallid version, a reporter merely describes the bleak economic conditions in Chicago and cites statistics on the number of jobs lost to the surrounding suburbs.[3]

Table 4.1 shows the importance participants ascribed to environmental hazards after having witnessed either a pallidly- or vividly-presented environmental horror story. The table reveals not a trace of the expected vividness effect. In fact, the composite ratings tilt slightly in the *opposite* direction. Participants who saw the vivid rendition of either the chemical waste site story or the story about asbestos contamination actually rated environmental hazards as a somewhat *less* serious problem than did their counterparts who watched the pallid versions of the same stories. The differences are admittedly small (in neither case can we be confident that the difference is real), but this hardly constitutes support for the vividness hypothesis. Moreover, matters improve only slightly for the hypothesis when we turn to the

TABLE 4.1

Importance of Environmental Hazards as a Function of Vividness of TV News Presentation: Experiment 6

Story	Measure of Importance	Presentation		Difference: Vivid Presentation Minus Pallid Presentation
		Pallid	Vivid	
Toxic wastes	Composite ratings	83	74	−09*
	Percentage naming	25	31	06
Asbestos contamination	Composite ratings	80	75	−05
	Percentage naming	25	25	00

*$p < .13$

national problems participants spontaneously nominate. As shown in table 4.1, environmental hazards are as likely to be mentioned in the aftermath of pallid presentations that deal in abstractions and statistics as in the wake of vivid stories that focus poignantly and powerfully on individual victims. All in all, these results amount to a rather crushing disconfirmation of the vividness hypothesis.

The results from the unemployment conditions of experiment 6, shown in table 4.2, also hold out little encouragement for a general vividness effect. The results are more interesting, however, since they indicate that vivid presentations can strengthen or weaken agenda-setting. Consistent with the vividness hypothesis, participants shown the vivid rendition of the story on cuts in the CETA program judged unemployment to be a more important problem (slightly and non-significantly) and were significantly more likely to name unemployment as one of the country's most important problems than those exposed to the pallid version. In contradiction to the vividness hypothesis, participants who viewed the vivid version of the story about unemployment in Chicago rated unemployment to be significantly *less* important and were significantly *less* likely to nominate unemployment as a national problem than those who watched the pallid presentation.

So all told, experiment 6 provides little support for a vividness bias. As a general matter, agenda-setting effects were not strengthened when news was presented vividly. Human despair and devastation, poignantly depicted, did not generally add to viewers' sense of national priorities.

TABLE 4.2

Importance of Unemployment as a Function of Vividness of TV News Presentation: Experiment 6

Story	Measure of Importance	Presentation		Difference: Vivid Presentation Minus Pallid Presentation
		Pallid	Vivid	
Chicago's West Side	Composite ratings	95	84	−11***
	Percentage naming	83	64	−19*
CETA cuts	Composite ratings	87	88	01
	Percentage naming	62	83	21**

$*p < .18$
$**p < .12$
$***p < .05$

Perhaps this reflects an admirable tough-mindedness and preference for logical reasoning on the public's part. After all, the significance attached to unemployment as a national problem should not depend on a single instance, however powerful and tragic it might be. Alternatively, the failure to confirm the vividness hypothesis in experiment 6 may reflect a flaw in design. It is nearly impossible to vary vividness of information without at the same time varying the content of information. In experiment 6, we created vivid and pallid versions of the *same* news story, in an attempt to hold as constant as possible the information conveyed by each. To the degree we failed to do so, our experimental results may reflect differences both in the vividness of presentation and in the substance of the news itself. It is possible that the pallid versions of the stories employed in experiment 6 contain more and more powerful information than do the vivid versions. Consequently, there may be vividness effects hiding in experiment 6, effects that were neutralized by the inadvertently powerful pallid presentations. We think this quite unlikely, but it remains a logical possibility, and one that we pursued in experiment 11. There we examined whether a vivid depiction of a single unemployed worker attached to a pallid account of unemployment nationwide would prove more influential than the pallid account alone.

Experiment 11 also took up in more systematic fashion a possibility hinted at by experiment 6. The most remarkable outcome in experiment 6 was not that vivid cases fail to enhance the influence of the evening news (though that was surprising enough) but rather that, under certain circumstances, vivid cases may actually diminish the capacity of the news to influence the public's political priorities. Participants in experiment 6 whose collection of news stories included the vivid version of hard times in Chicago watched a young man searching for work. They concluded, compared to their counterparts exposed to the pallid version of the same story, that unemployment was not such an important problem. Participants whose collection included the vivid presentation of cuts in CETA witnessed an emotional conversation with a middle-aged father of two children, who declared that without CETA, "I'd still be walking the streets." They concluded, compared to their counterparts in the pallid rendition, that unemployment was indeed a very important problem.[4] How might this sharp contrast be explained?

The two stories differ in many respects, of course, but perhaps most consequentially, they differ in the race of the victim. The young man searching for a job in Chicago was black; the middle-aged father of two dependent on CETA was white. By varying the race of the victim, we may have inadvertently manipulated the effectiveness of the story.

Ninety percent of the participants in experiment 6 were white. Many may have felt little sympathy for the black victim. If the story's actual effect was to evoke racial stereotypes, then news about hard times for blacks in Chicago might have been typically understood not as news about unemployment, but as further confirmation that blacks lack the skill or motivation necessary to find and then hold onto jobs. Many whites may think the blacks are not the victims of unemployment, but that they deserve it. Or, in a more charitable interpretation, white viewers may have regarded information about the plight of an unemployed black man in Chicago as irrelevant to the nation's economic predicament. Unemployment may be a grave problem for young urban blacks, but not for the country as a whole. In short, the vividness effect as we have pursued it here may be contingent on the affinity between victim and viewer. It was this possibility that we pursued in experiment 11.

Experiment 11 was run in Ann Arbor in April of 1983 with University of Michigan undergraduates as participants. We assembled three collections of news stories, identical in all respects but for one story about unemployment. Participants assigned to the first treatment condition saw a news story that presented the latest national statistics on unemployment, which indicated an increase in the number of unemployed Americans. In the other two conditions, participants saw exactly the same story, but this time it was followed (as part of the same story) by an interview with a specific victim of unemployment. In one the victim was white, in the other he was black.

As a first move, we compared judgments about unemployment expressed by those who saw the pallid presentation only against those expressed by participants who saw both statistics and individual victims. In this analysis we combine the black and white victim conditions, since we are interested in the possibility of a *general* vividness bias. The results, shown in table 4.3, support this possibility not at all.

TABLE 4.3

Importance of Unemployment as a Function of Vividness of TV News Presentation: Experiment 11

Measure of Importance	Presentation		Difference: Vivid Presentation Minus Pallid Presentation
	Pallid	Vivid	
Composite ratings	85	84	−01
Percentage naming	91	63	−28*

*$p < .01$

Viewers presented with statistics and vivid cases rated unemployment no more important than did those presented with statistics alone, and were actually significantly *less* likely to cite unemployment as one of the country's most important problems. Once again, we uncover no support for a general vividness bias. As in experiment 6, adding a vivid case seems, if anything, to diminish the power of television news to set the public's agenda.

We have argued that vivid presentations may fail most completely when they depict victims that differ in obvious ways from viewers. Race, of course, supplies an especially obvious distinction and often an invidious one. Consistent with this line of argument, white viewers did indeed attach greater national significance to unemployment after having witnessed a white person struggling with joblessness than after witnessing a black person with similar troubles: they concluded that unemployment was a more serious problem and were more apt to nominate unemployment as among the country's most important problems (these results are shown in table 4.4). The differences are not dramatic, but they are consistent with our expectations and with the results from experiment 6.

We can carry this analysis one step further, since in experiment 11 we assessed participants' attitudes toward blacks.[5] We expected that the racial differences just noted would widen among those white viewers least sympathetic to blacks. This expectation is supported in table 4.5. Among viewers who offered unfavorable evaluations of blacks, the race of the victim made a large difference; among those who indicated favorable evaluations of blacks, the race of the victim proved largely irrelevant. After exposure to national statistics documenting an increase in unemployment and one *black* man's struggles with job loss, viewers unsympathetic to blacks rated unemployment as a less serious problem and were much less likely to name unemployment as one of

TABLE 4.4

Importance of Unemployment as a Function of Race of Victim Portrayed in TV News Story: Experiment 11

Measure of Importance	Race of Victim		Difference: White Victim Condition Minus Black Victim Condition
	Black	White	
Composite ratings	79	88	09*
Percentage naming	53	71	18**

*$p < .07$
**$p < .13$

TABLE 4.5

Importance of Unemployment as a Function of Race of Victim Portrayed in TV News Story, and Viewer's Attitude toward Blacks: Experiment 11

Measure of Importance	Attitude toward Blacks	Race of Victim		Difference: White Victim Presentation Minus Black Victim Presentation
		Black	White	
Composite ratings	Favorable	81	75	−06
	Unfavorable	67	77	10**
Percentage naming	Favorable	63	54	−09
	Unfavorable	57	91	34*

*$p < .15$ (race of victim × attitude toward blacks interaction)

**$p < .08$ (race of victim × attitude toward blacks interaction)

the nation's most pressing problems than after exposure to the same statistics followed by one *white* man's unemployment struggles.

To summarize: Experiments 6 and 11 suggest that, contrary to much conventional wisdom, news stories that direct viewers' attention to the flesh and blood victims of national problems prove no more persuasive than news stories that cover national problems impersonally—indeed, they tend to be *less* persuasive. This undermining of agenda-setting may be particularly powerful when viewers in effect blame the victims for the problems that have befallen them. Perhaps vivid presentations are generally less persuasive in part because they are so successful as melodrama. Viewers may get so caught up in one family's troubles that they fail to make the connection back to the national condition. Overwhelmed by concrete details, they miss the general point.

THE LEAD STORY HYPOTHESIS

Although stories that traffic in personal case histories do not generally enhance agenda-setting, stories that appear at the top of the broadcast may. The networks carefully select the lead story to represent the day's most important news item (Gans 1979). Perhaps viewers recognize and endorse this editorial judgment. If so, lead stories should be more powerful in shaping viewers' priorities about the importance of national problems than stories that appear elsewhere in the newscast.

To test the lead story hypothesis, we conducted experiment 14 in New Haven in August 1983. Each of this assemblage experiment's four conditions consisted of an entire thirty-minute national newscast, complete with commercials. Participants were recruited in the usual way and informed that they were to watch a randomly selected news program that had been broadcast during the past month. Two of the conditions included a story on governmental attempts to halt drug smuggling. In the first version, the story on drug smuggling led off the broadcast; in the second, the story appeared roughly midway through the broadcast. The second two conditions included a story on the difficulties facing public schools, once again positioned either at the top of the broadcast or in the middle. Experiment 14 therefore allows us to test the lead story hypothesis twice, once with illicit drugs and once with public education as the target problem. Since in each instance, participants are exposed to exactly the same information, we can tell whether the editorial decision to place one story at the beginning of the broadcast, by itself, affects viewers' priorities.[6]

As in other assemblage experiments, participants were questioned immediately after the broadcast. Their answers are summarized in table 4.6. As shown there, the story that described government efforts to curtail the flow of illegal drugs into the United States was substantially more influential in the lead position than when it appeared in the middle of the broadcast, on both indicators of importance. When the story led off the news, illicit drugs was rated a more significant national problem and was more often named as one of the most important problems facing the country. The account of the troubles experienced by public schools in the United States was also more influential in the lead position on both measures of importance, as table 4.6 indicates. Neither difference was large enough to reach statistical significance, however. So the overall pattern is mixed: when stories begin the broadcast, they are more influential than they otherwise would be; precisely how much more influential may depend on the nature of the story itself.

To pursue the lead story effect further, we pursued our participants

TABLE 4.6
Problem Importance as a Function of Target Story's Position in TV News Broadcast (Immediate posttest): Experiment 14

Problem	Measure of Importance	Story's Position		Difference: Lead Position Minus Middle Position
		Middle	Lead	
Drugs	Composite ratings	54	68	14**
	Percentage naming	4	17	13*
Education	Composite ratings	78	80	02
	Percentage naming	10	12	02

*$p < .05$
**$p < .02$

further. One week after the completion of the experiment, all participants were mailed a second questionnaire. Many of our standard measures of problem importance were of course included, sprinkled
among various filler questions about news programs and television reporters. Eighty-three of the original 121 participants completed and
returned this second questionnaire (69 percent), affording us an opportunity to examine the persistence or decay of the lead story effect.[7]

The results, displayed in table 4.7, contain several surprises. The
biggest is the emergence of substantial delayed lead story effects on
judgments of the importance of public education, where the immediate effects were so modest. Now, one week after having watched a lead
story on the decline of public schools, participants regarded education
as a substantially more serious problem and were more apt to name it
as one of the nation's most important problems compared to those who
saw the same story in the middle of the broadcast. This constitutes unexpectedly strong support for the lead story hypothesis. In the case of
the story about drug trafficking, lead story effects diminished. One
week later, viewers who had seen the story in the lead position continued to regard drug smuggling as a more serious national problem
than did viewers exposed to the identical story in the middle of the
broadcast, but the differences narrowed over what it had been immediately following the presentation. Moreover, viewers in the lead story
condition were actually *less* likely to mention drugs as an important
national problem one week later than were viewers in the middle position condition, though this difference cannot be confidently distinguished from zero.

Considered together, the results from experiment 14 are more ir-
regular than we would like, and the irregularities seem, at least to us,

TABLE 4.7

Problem Importance as a Function of Target Story's Position in TV News Broadcast
(Delayed posttest): Experiment 14

Problem	Measure of Importance	Story's Position		Difference: Lead Position Minus Middle Position
		Middle	Lead	
Drugs	Composite ratings	53	66	13**
	Percentage naming	18	7	−11
Education	Composite ratings	71	84	13***
	Percentage naming	18	33	15*

  *$p < .12$
 **$p < .06$
***$p < .01$

quite mysterious. Nevertheless, we believe the results convey a general lesson, and that is the special effectiveness of lead stories. Stories that appear first tend to matter more.

To validate this result, we again moved outside the laboratory, returning to our analysis of national public opinion surveys described in chapter 3. In addition to recording the total number of news stories regarding energy, inflation, and unemployment broadcast by CBS between 1974 and 1980, we also counted the number of lead stories and the number of nonlead stories devoted to each of the three problems. This permits us to estimate whatever special impact lead stories might have on the priorities the public attached to energy, inflation, and unemployment. To do so requires only that we reestimate the equations reported in Chapter 3, this time including both the number of lead stories and the number of nonlead stories as separate predictors of the public's priorities.[8]

The results are clear: we find very strong effects on public opinion due to lead stories, independent of the effects due to nonlead stories. For every lead story broadcast on energy, public responses citing energy as one of the country's most important problems increased by about 1 percent (this result along with those that follow can be found in Appendix B). Roughly the same result held for inflation. With respect to unemployment, three lead stories were required to boost public concern about unemployment one percentage point. These are substantial effects. Moreover, once they are taken into account, it is hard to find any effects due to news stories that appear elsewhere. According to these results, virtually all of the change in the public's concern over energy, inflation, and unemployment that is produced by alterations in television coverage can be traced to lead story coverage. Our analysis of national surveys therefore buttresses considerably the case made by experiment 14. Both affirm the importance of the editorial act by which lead stories are selected.

CONCLUSION

We have probed a bit deeper into agenda-setting in this chapter, albeit with mixed success. On the one hand, as expected, stories positioned at the top of the broadcast are those that carry the networks' agenda most effectively. The time-series survey evidence suggests that lead stories dominate the agenda-setting process. The experimental evidence suggests that at least part of this effect is due not to substance but to form: lead stories are effective in part simply because they lead off the broadcast. This result may reflect viewers' endorsement of the networks' editorial judgment. In this view, lead stories matter more because viewers, taking their cues from the networks, confer special significance upon them. Alternatively and more crudely, lead stories may owe their advantage just to being first. In this view, lead stories are especially effective because they appear before the viewer's mind begins to wander.

On the other hand, counter to our expectations, we found no support for the vividness hypothesis. Personal cases that illustrate national problems in poignant and powerful ways typically do not add to agenda-setting. Indeed, they often undermine agenda-setting, particularly when viewers regard the vividly-portrayed cases as not entirely innocent, as somehow implicated in their own troubles. These results certainly put an ironic twist on the great political commotion stirred up by "People Like Us." As melodrama—as a powerful and moving account of *particular Americans* in desperate straits—"People Like Us" can only be judged a great success. But as a political statement—as a portrait of *the nation's* problems—the documentary may have succeeded not at all.

Vividness can be defined in many ways and we have considered only one. Our results do not argue against vividness effects in general; they indicate only that dramatic vignettes of personal suffering do not enhance agenda-setting. Although limited in scope, this conclusion is nevertheless important, not the least because dramatic personal vignettes constitute a common currency by which television news achieves, by some accounts, its highest calling: the communication not of information or analysis but of raw human experience.

Personal Predicaments and National Problems

For millions of Americans, national problems are also pressing personal problems. Crime, unemployment, and racial discrimination occur not only out in society but also in everyday life. It is one thing to learn from the CBS Evening News that serious crime is on the increase in the United States; quite another to be mugged on the way to the corner grocery store. In reaching judgments about national problems, how do Americans take into account these very different types of evidence—evidence from television news, on the one hand, and from their personal experiences, on the other?

PERSONAL PREDICAMENTS AND POLITICAL JUDGMENTS: ASSUMPTIONS AND EVIDENCE

It is practically an article of faith that political judgments reflect personal predicaments in a direct and immediate way. Surely Americans assess the course of national affairs partly by considering the circumstances of their own lives. Surely their views of national life are conditioned and colored by what happens to them.

In fact, the connection between personal life and political judgment appears to be surprisingly weak. Consider the following examples, drawn from a variety of domains. Victims of crimes do not typically regard crime as a more serious problem for society as a whole or even for their own communities than do those personally untouched by crime (Tyler 1980; Kinder and Sears 1981). Americans whose personal lives were most disrupted by the severe energy shortages of 1974 were no more likely to believe the energy crisis to be a serious and persistent national problem than were those whose personal lives were untouched (Sears, Tyler, Citrin, and Kinder 1978). The war in Vietnam loomed no larger as a political problem among those who had close relatives that served there than among Americans without such personal connections to the war (Lau, Brown, and Sears 1978). White Americans personally affected by racial busing programs generally do not take more extreme opinions on that issue than those taken by white Americans unaffected by such programs (Kinder and Sears 1981; Kinder and Rhodebeck 1981). Americans' assessments of the economic condition of their society are distinct from the economic setbacks and achievements they encounter in their own lives (Kinder and Kiewiet 1981; Kinder, Adams, and Gronke 1985; Kiewiet 1983; Sears and Citrin 1982). In short, Americans seem to distinguish sharply between the quality of their personal lives on the one hand and the quality of national life on the other. Personal predicaments are consequential and preoccupying—but they remain, for the most part, *personal*. They contribute rather little to beliefs about society or the nation.

But perhaps personal predicaments play a more subtle role in the judgments Americans develop regarding the condition of their society. It seems self-evident that the priorities people attach to national problems are determined both by the news coverage they are exposed to and by their readiness to absorb such coverage. Readiness no doubt has a variety of sources, but a most important one may be personal circumstances. Following Erbring, Goldenberg, and Miller (1980), we suggest that people who are personally affected by a particular problem are more likely to be sensitive to news about it—they are predisposed to accept the news that *their* problem is a serious one for the country—and are therefore especially susceptible to media influence.[1] We test this suggestion here by examining how the predicaments of personal life interact with television coverage of the nation's condition in determining Americans' views of national problems.

TESTING THE IMPACT OF PERSONAL PREDICAMENTS

The separate and interactive effects of personal predicaments and news coverage were assessed in experiment 5, conducted in assemblage style in New Haven during August and September of 1981. Experiment 5 concentrated on three problems: civil rights, unemployment, and social security. Participants were exposed either to intermediate (two stories) or extensive (four stories) coverage of one of the three target problems and saw no news of the other two. Personal predicament was treated as a simple dichotomy: victims of racial discrimination, unemployment, or the threatened collapse of the social security system were compared with those not so affected. Thus, one-half of the participants in the civil rights treatment were employed blacks; half of the participants in the unemployment treatment were unemployed white males; half of the viewers in the social security treatment were white senior citizens. The remaining participants in each treatment were made up equally of the two groups not affected by the target problem.

The news stories making up the treatments were originally broadcast during 1980 and 1981. Stories about civil rights depicted racial disparities in income and attempts by the federal government and civil rights organizations to promote racial equality. Stories about unemployment focused on increases in the unemployment rate nationwide and the impact of unemployment on particular communities and families. Stories about social security, finally, dealt with congressional attempts to avoid a financial collapse of the system and with the economic plight of the elderly.

The effect of personal predicaments and news coverage on the importance viewers assigned to various national problems is shown in table 5.1. The table displays, for civil rights, unemployment, and social security, the percentage of participants naming the problem as one of the country's most important at each of three levels of news coverage (zero, two, or four stories) and at each of two levels of personal predicament (for those personally affected or personally unaffected by the problem).[2]

In light of the empirical returns from previous research, the results from experiment 5 contain some surprises. Most notably table 5.1 reveals, for two of the three problems, very substantial effects associated with personal predicaments. Consider just the first column of the table, which includes those participants who saw no news about "their" problem. As shown there, blacks were much more likely to mention civil rights than were whites: 47 percent of the black participants spontaneously named civil rights as a serious national problem as compared to just 7 percent of the white participants. Similarly, saving the social security system was much more likely to be cited by the elderly than by the young: 19 percent of the elderly named social security as against

TABLE 5.1

Problem Importance as a Function of Intensity of TV News Coverage and Viewer's Personal Situation

Percentage Naming Problem as One of Country's Most Important: Experiment 5

Problem	Personal Situation	Number of Stories			Difference: 4 stories minus 0 stories
		0	2	4	
Civil rights	Black	47	38	67	20
	White	7	22	0	− 7
Unemployment	Unemployed	36	25	100	64
	Employed	29	33	46	17
Social security	Elderly	19	67	50	31
	Young	4	13	38	34

just 4 percent of the young. In contrast (and more in keeping with pre-vious research), victims of unemployment were only slightly more likely to name unemployment as one of the country's most important problems than were the employed: 36 percent vs. 29 percent.[3]

Table 5.1 also reveals how television news fares in competition with personal predicaments. In some ways, of course, this is an unfair con-test, since a few minutes spent casually in front of a television screen would seem no match for a lifetime's accumulation of experience with racial discrimination, the personal devastation that accompanies losing a job, or the bleak financial realities facing the elderly at the prospect of cutbacks in social security. Nevertheless, as the table shows, news coverage generally did have an impact. As coverage increased (from left to right across the table), so too did the percentage of viewers nam-ing the problem. The differences are not dramatic (they fail in the case of civil rights to achieve statistical significance), but it would be unre-alistic to expect them to be.

The most interesting evidence furnished by experiment 5 concerns the possible interaction between personal predicaments and news cov-erage. We had anticipated that the impact of television news would be more pronounced among those personally affected by the problem given coverage. The results in table 5.1 support this expectation in all three cases. News about civil rights was more influential among blacks than among whites; news about unemployment was more influential among the unemployed than among the employed; and news about so-cial security was more influential among the elderly than among the young.[4]

To convince ourselves that these results were not a happy accident, we undertook experiment 9. Experiment 9 focused on a single prob-lem—unemployment—and was conducted in New Haven during Au-gust of 1982. Over the course of a week, experimental participants watched a series of national news broadcasts into which we inserted stories about unemployment: seven stories inserted into four newscasts for a total of fourteen minutes. Roughly half of the participants were employed on a full-time basis; half were unemployed. We also recruited an additional set of participants to serve as a control group. These par-ticipants completed the posttest questionnaire a few days after those in the experimental group and were evenly divided between the em-ployed and the unemployed.[5] The control and experimental groups did not differ with respect to standard social and economic background characteristics, nor did they differ in their interest in and attention to politics.[6]

The results, shown in table 5.2, confirm our earlier findings in two

TABLE 5.2

Unemployment Importance as a Function of Intensity of TV News Coverage and Viewer's Personal Situation

Percentage Naming Unemployment as One of Country's Most Important Problems: Experiment 9

Personal Situation	Number of Stories		Difference: 7 stories minus 0 stories
	0	7	
Unemployed	71	81	10
Employed	53	90	37

respects but disconfirm them in another. As was the case in experiment 5, the unemployed in experiment 9 were not much more likely to name unemployment as a serous national problem than were the employed. Among control group participants who saw no news about unemployment, 71 percent of the unemployed named unemployment, while 53 percent of the employed did so, a difference that we cannot confidently distinguish from no difference at all.[7] And as in experiment 5, news coverage clearly made a difference: participants who watched the stories on unemployment that we had inserted into the broadcasts ended up naming unemployment as a serious national problem more frequently than those who saw no such stories (86 percent vs. 63 percent).[8] However, unlike the findings of experiment 5, the impact of stories about unemployment was *not* greater among the unemployed. Quite the reverse, in fact. In experiment 9, news coverage had a greater impact on the employed than on the unemployed.[9] We will return to this puzzle momentarily.

Conclusions

The predicaments of personal life can contribute directly and powerfully to the priorities Americans assign to national problems. According to our results, blacks attach much more significance to civil rights than whites do; the elderly worry much more about the health of the social security system than do the young. Although these results seem utterly straightforward, they are not. They contrast dramatically with the faint connections typically reported by previous research on the relationship between the predicaments of private life and judgments about national life. This contrast may reflect the distinctiveness of civil rights and social security as political problems.

We suspect that the key feature distinguishing civil rights and social security from other problems is that they are experienced psychologically both as personal and as group predicaments. Racial discrimination is directed at an entire class of people. Similarly, the threatened collapse of the social security system affects an entire cohort. Whereas the victims of unemployment may regard themselves as unfortunate *individuals,* victims of racial discrimination or government bankruptcy are more likely to regard themselves as members of unfortunate *groups.* This perception may lead to group identification, mobilization and eventually, perhaps, to political action (Miller, Gurin, Gurin, and Malanchuk 1981). It may also, as our evidence suggests, enable Americans to see the problems they face in their own lives as legitimate and serious problems for their country.[10]

Our results also show that personal predicaments can make viewers both *more* and *less* susceptible to news coverage. In experiment 5, news coverage of unemployment was more powerful among the unemployed; coverage of racial discrimination was more powerful among blacks; coverage of problems in the social security system was more powerful among the elderly. In experiment 9, however, news coverage of unemployment was more powerful among the employed. So personal predicaments matter, but sometimes they strengthen agenda-setting and sometimes they weaken it.

Perhaps this curious and unanticipated reversal can be understood by recognizing that political problems have their own life histories (cf. Downs 1972; Erbring, Goldenberg, and Miller 1980). By accident rather than design, we happened to undertake a pair of experiments at two different stages in the evolution of unemployment as a national problem. Experiment 5 was conducted in the fall of 1981, when unemployment was running at less than 8 percent, and when, according to a Gallup Poll undertaken at the time, Americans were much more concerned about inflation than they were about unemployment. Experiment 9 was conducted in July of 1982, during the depths of a recession, with the unemployment rate approaching 10 percent, and with, again according to Gallup, more than 60 percent of the American public naming unemployment or the recession as the most important problem facing the nation. Thus the two experiments provide snapshots of the agenda-setting process at two opposite stages. The first, taken at a time of moderate unemployment and high inflation, shows the unemployed altering their judgments more readily in response to news about unemployment. The second, taken following a period of extensive and prolonged unemployment, shows the employed to be influenced more by news about unemployment.

Taken together, these results suggest that when problems flare up and capture the attention of the media, agenda-setting effects show up most immediately among those directly affected by the problem. In this way, television news reinforces and ratifies the experiences of everyday life. But if coverage continues and the problem stays at the top of the media's agenda (as unemployment did through the first half of 1982), agenda-setting effects will begin to register just as deeply among those viewers whose personal lives are untroubled by the problems given national attention. Eventually such viewers may actually be influenced more by additional coverage than are the problems' real victims, whose concern may have reached maximal levels. This means that for those problems that burst upon the political scene, appearing without warning and disappearing just as suddenly, agenda-setting effects will be greatest among those whose personal lives are directly affected.[11] For problems with more staying power, however, though the personally affected may react more rapidly, the rest of the public may eventually catch up.

At a more general level, the experiments described here document the perhaps unremarkable fact that the impact of news coverage—the strength of the agenda-setting effect—depends in part on the characteristics of the audience. Viewers personally acquainted with a particular problem are more susceptible to news coverage of that problem early in the problem's life history and are, perhaps, less susceptible to coverage later on. This is an important result, but the predicaments of personal life are just one way to define variation in the audience. In the next chapter, we broaden our investigation of viewer characteristics that render them more or less vulnerable to the images and information that flicker across their television screens.

Victims of Agenda-Setting

The experimental results reported in the preceding chapter show that the impact of television news coverage depends partly on the particular life circumstances of those who watch. In this chapter we broaden our inquiry beyond the personal predicaments of private life to examine in a more general way characteristics of viewers that make them more or less susceptible to television's view of the world. We entertain three possibilities in particular: that agenda-setting will diminish among the well-educated and will increase among the poorly-educated; that agenda-setting will diminish among strong partisans and increase among political independents; and that agenda-setting will diminish among those most deeply involved in politics and increase among those whose involvements lie elsewhere. We focus on these three characteristics—education, partisanship, and political involvement—because, as an empirical matter, no other characteristics are so regularly and powerfully correlated with the opinions Americans express about politics. Here we will see whether education, partisanship, and involvement condition agenda-setting, as they condition so much else of Americans' political behavior.

Education, Party Identification and Political Involvement as Key Characteristics

Education

Education is an excellent place to begin, because

there is probably no single variable in the survey repertoire that generates as substantial correlations in such a variety of directions in political behavior material as level of formal education. Whether one is dealing with cognitive matters such as level of factual information about politics or conceptual sophistication in its assessment; or such motivational matters as degree of attention paid to politics and emotional involvement in political affairs; or questions of actual behavior, such as engagement in any of a variety of political activities from party work to vote turnout itself; education is everywhere the universal solvent, and the relationship is always in the same direction. The educated citizen is attentive, knowledgeable, and participatory, and the uneducated citizen is not (Converse 1972, 324).

Given these stark differences, education may also make a difference for agenda-setting. If the better-educated are more sophisticated and critical, then perhaps their political views are less malleable in general and therefore less susceptible to agenda-setting in particular.[1]

PARTY IDENTIFICATION

Most Americans develop attachments to one of the major political parties relatively early in adult life and then cling to them rather tenaciously (Kinder and Sears 1985). Such attachments represent a kind of cognitive resource: they offer to voters an efficient way to impose order and meaning on the disorderly and confusing world of politics. As Stokes put it:

> To the average person the affairs of government are remote and complex, and yet the average citizen is asked periodically to formulate opinions about these affairs. At the very least he has to decide how he will vote, what choice he will make between candidates offering different programs and very different versions of contemporary political events. In this dilemma, having the party symbol stamped on certain candidates, certain issue positions, certain interpretations of political reality is of great psychological convenience (1966, 126–27).

Of course, not everyone is a devoted Democrat or Republican. Independents who look at the political world without the cognitive benefits of a partisan lens may as a consequence be more vulnerable to the views of national life conveyed by the networks.[2]

POLITICAL INVOLVEMENT

Americans vary enormously in their involvement in politics. Some express a keen interest in political events, voraciously consume great numbers of newspapers, magazines, and television programs devoted to public affairs, talk incessantly about politics with their friends, volunteer their time and money to campaigns, and know a great deal about politics. Others—the vast majority of us—are far less involved. Here we consider whether such differences in involvement condition the viewer's susceptibility to agenda-setting. In doing so, we examine five related but separable aspects of involvement.

The first and most general is *political interest*. We want to know first of all whether the strength of the agenda-setting effect varies as a function of the interest viewers express in politics. To get at this, we asked participants two questions: how closely they followed government and public affairs, and (among those who claimed to read a daily newspaper regularly) how much attention they paid to news about government and politics in their daily newspapers.[3]

A second aspect of involvement particularly relevant to our research is *media exposure*. We asked participants whether they read a daily newspaper and how often 'they watched the network's national newscasts.[4] The first measure is important, since it seems reasonable to expect that people who are dependent on multiple sources of information will be less influenced by any single source. The second measure is also important, but for a different reason. If we were to find, for example, that our experimental demonstrations of agenda-setting were confined entirely to people who ordinarily *never* watch network news (to consider one horrifying possibility), our results would lose much of their force. We would then have demonstrated an agenda-setting effect with a population that, under ordinary circumstances, never encounters television news.

A third aspect of involvement is participation in *informal communication* about politics. Discussions with family members, friends, neighbors, and coworkers constitute an alternative source on public affairs that may override the influence of media in general and television news in particular. Erbring, Goldenberg, and Miller put this point strongly:

Getting at the meaning of the news involves assessing its implications for the future, tracing developments from the past, comparing current events with previous experience, weighing the credibility of particular sources, and so forth. It calls, in short, for an *interpretation* of the news—not by individual intuition but by "social reality testing." Informal communication with others is essential to help people make sense of news media content, and thus plays a critical role in shaping public perceptions of issue salience (1980, 40–41).

To assess this possibility, we asked participants how often they discussed political topics with friends and acquaintances.[5]

A fourth aspect of political involvement is *activism*. Some Americans are political whirlwinds—they volunteer for campaigns, mobilize their neighbors to influence city hall, pressure public officials, and vote religiously. Meanwhile, most of the rest of us, more often than not, stay home. Do such differences matter for agenda-setting? To find out, we asked participants whether they had recently engaged in five separate political activities and then summed their answers to form an index of activism.[6]

The fifth and final aspect of involvement we consider is *expertise*. By expertise we refer to the amount of political information individuals command. Although some Americans know a great deal about national defense, for instance, others know scarcely anything at all. This difference reflects variations in problem expertise. Experts not only know more about a particular problem, their knowledge is better organized. As a consequence, experts may possess a greater and more flexible ability to deal with new information. While experts may be free to examine the news more deeply and perhaps more critically, novices may have their minds occupied just coming to terms with what is being said, leaving them open to influence. Our measure of expertise is problem-specific: we asked a set of questions to measure expertise for each national problem whose coverage was systematically varied in our experiments.[7]

As the preceding discussion implies, education, party identification, and political involvement can be thought of as resources. Education indicates general cognitive and analytical abilities. Party identification offers a convenient and economical way to organize and understand the political world. Involvement summarizes a rich and diverse set of political experiences. These resources may be considered as competitors to television news. For the well-educated, partisan, and the involved, television news is but one of several sources of information. Heading into the analysis, therefore, our expectation was that the power of television news would diminish among viewers rich in such resources: i.e., we predicted that agenda-setting will be weakest among the well-educated, the partisan, and the politically involved.

ANALYSIS AND RESULTS

To see whether this was so, we returned again to the sequential experiments described in previous chapters: experiments 2, 8, and 9 (we excluded experiment 1 since it contained neither the open-ended "most important national problem" question nor measures of problem expertise). Together, experiments 2, 8, and 9 cover six different national problems: defense, inflation, unemployment, nuclear arms control, civil rights, and pollution. In the analysis that follows, we combine the three experiments and proceed to analyze the results as if they had been generated by one large experiment devoted to a single target problem. So for participants exposed to news about inflation in experiment 2, we analyze changes in beliefs about inflation; for those exposed to news about civil rights in experiment 8, we analyze changes in beliefs about civil rights; and so on.[8] As before, the magnitude of agenda-setting is gauged by the amount of change in participants' composite ratings of problem importance, and by the extent to which those participants who failed to mention the target problem as among the country's most important before watching the newscasts did so after exposure to the edited newscasts. In both cases, the greater the change, the greater the impact of the news.

In prior analyses, we have been concerned primarily with change in the aggregate, averaged across different types of viewers. Now we wish to take a closer look at change, to see whether television coverage is especially influential among viewers with fewer political resources. Insofar as political resources determine viewers' susceptibility to agenda-setting, changes in beliefs about the importance of political problems should be particularly pronounced among those with little formal education, with no attachment to a political party, and with scant involvement in politics. Viewer characteristics were examined one at a time; first education, then partisanship, and finally, the several aspects of involvement (technical details concerning the analysis are given in Appendix B).

Table 6.1 displays the results. The first column indicates whether change in participants' composite ratings of problem importance varies by education, party identification, and involvement. The second column provides the same information for participants spontaneously mentioning national problems. The entry of .54 in the table's first col-

TABLE 6.1

Change in Problem Importance Induced by TV News Coverage among Different Types of Viewers: Experiments 2, 8, and 9 Combined

	Composite Ratings	Spontaneous Mentions
Education		
High school or less	.54**	.28
Party Identification		
Independent	.62**	.58*
Involvement		
Follows public affairs rarely	.84**	.41
Pays little attention to newspaper coverage of politics	.32	.80*
Doesn't read a daily newspaper	−.17	.06
Watches TV news rarely	.15	.68**
Discusses politics rarely	.25	.38
Politically inactive	.99**	.91**
No expertise	−.01	.02

** $p < .01$ * $p < .05$

Note: The first column table entries are unstandardized two-stage least squares coefficients; the second column entries are logit coefficients (see Appendix B for technical details). A positive coefficient means that the agenda-setting effect is more pronounced among viewers of the type specified. Positive coefficients are predicted in all instances.

umn and first row thus means that agenda-setting (defined by change in composite ratings) was that much greater among the poorly-educated (participants with high school education or less) than among the well-educated (those with at least some college), a difference that achieves statistical significance.

We had expected to find positive coefficients—meaning that those with few political resources are swayed most by the network agenda—and generally we did. Of the eighteen coefficients displayed in table 6.1, just two are negative and neither of those can be reliably distinguished from zero. As anticipated, viewers with little formal schooling were influenced more than the well-educated; independents more than partisans; the politically lethargic more than the politically involved. This pattern held both for shifts in ratings of problem importance and for changes in the spontaneous listing of the nation's most important problems. Indeed, the degree of convergence across the two measures of agenda-setting is striking.

Table 6.1 does provide a few surprises, however. Although interest in politics and particularly actual participation in politics showed the expected relationship, other aspects of involvement seemed generally irrelevant to the magnitude of agenda-setting. Television news coverage was generally just as effective among those who read a daily newspaper as among those who did not; among those who talked about politics with their friends frequently as those who did so infrequently; among those who knew a lot about the problem given coverage as those who knew little; and among those who watched network news regularly as among those who watched rarely. The last nonresult listed here is, of course, of special interest. It suggests that our agenda-setting results are generally not confined to "nonwatchers"—to people whose entire acquaintance with the evening news comes from participating in our experiment.

Education, party identification, and involvement are themselves correlated, of course. Those with less schooling also tend to be less engaged by politics; partisans tend to take a more active role in campaigns than do independents; and so forth.[9] Moreover, education, partisanship, and involvement also tend to be correlated with other variables that could conceivably be related to an individual viewer's susceptibility to the news. Consequently, we need to supplement the analysis reported so far, which takes up the effects of a single political resource at a time, with a multivariate analysis. The strength of this approach is that it estimates the separate and independent effect due to each political resource, holding constant the effects due to all others.

The results of the multivariate analysis largely sustain those reported so far (details are provided in Appendix B). As before, the characteristics of the viewer that matter most are partisanship, interest, and activism. The one material change is that in the multivariate analysis, the impact of education fades to the vanishing point. Thus while our original analysis indicated that the well-educated are influenced less than are the poorly-educated, the multivariate analysis indicates that it is not education per se that is responsible for this difference. Whatever special cognitive and analytical abilities education may breed constitute no defense against agenda-setting. If the well-educated are less influenced, it is because of their greater partisanship, interest, and activism. These constitute the effective resources for resisting agenda-setting.

CONCLUSIONS

The power of television news to set the public agenda depends partly on *which* public we have in mind. Television coverage is particularly effective in shaping the judgments of citizens with limited political resources and skills. Those who rarely get caught up in the world of politics find network news presentations particularly compelling. Partisans, activists, close observers of the political scene, on the other hand, are less apt to be swept away. The more removed the viewer is from the world of public affairs, the stronger the agenda-setting power of television news.

Defenders of democracy who regard television news as a sinister force may be tempted to take comfort in these results. From this point of view, perhaps it is a good thing that those Americans who are influenced the most by television news participate in politics the least. Thank goodness, they might say, that those whose political views are most drastically formed and reformed by television news do so little to make those views felt. This conclusion should be resisted, however, since the implications of our experimental results require a more complicated story.

The story is more complicated because for the first time our experimental results fail to be fully corroborated by findings from survey research. We find the politically engaged to be less responsive to experimentally-induced alterations in the media's agenda; analysts of public opinion, in contrast, often find just the reverse. To be sure, it is most accurate to say that on this point, the survey evidence is mixed. Some researchers find, as we do in our experiments, that the politically engaged are the least vulnerable to agenda-setting (e.g., Weaver, Graber, McCombs, and Eyal 1981). But the balance of the evidence (and the evidence we find more persuasive) is on the other side, indicating that the politically engaged are the most responsive to change in the media's agenda (e.g., MacKuen 1981, 1984). This result obviously diverges from our own. How can the two be reconciled?

One answer makes use of the distinctions often drawn in information-processing accounts of attitude change, between the initial reception of a message, on the one hand, and acceptance of its conclusions, on the other.[10] Attitude change requires both reception and acceptance: the power of television news to set the public's agenda testifies to its capacity to reach a wide audience (reception) with pictures and words that many find compelling (acceptance). The distinction is pertinent here because, as McGuire (1968) points out, characteristics of the audience may often be related in *opposite* ways to the two stages of processing and hence exert complex and situationally-dependent effects on overall change.

A case in point is political involvement. Political involvement may be *positively* related to reception and *negatively* related to acceptance. Whereas the politically involved may be more likely to tune in and pay close attention to television news coverage, they may be less likely to be persuaded by the coverage since their views are more firmly anchored. This means that the relationship between involvement and agenda-setting may be positive or negative, depending on the situation. In our experiments, where everyone, regardless of political interest, is exposed to the broadcasts, the negative relationship between involvement and acceptance may dominate the overall relationship. Consequently, we find that the politically engaged are typically influenced less than the politically indifferent, who possess fewer resources for resistance. But where exposure to television news is completely voluntary, the positive relationship between involvement and reception may dominate the overall relationship. Consequently, survey researchers typically find that the politically engaged are influenced more than the politically indifferent, because the engaged are much more likely to notice when the agenda actually has changed (see, especially, MacKuen 1984).

In short, the experimental results reported in this chapter may be quite misleading if interpreted as identifying pockets of the public that are most responsive to changes in network news coverage. Our results speak instead primarily to the acceptance stage of the agenda-setting process. They pertain primarily to the *capacity* of television news to influence opinion among different sorts of people, should those people be tuning in with roughly equal attention.

In this respect, it is significant that the agenda-setting capacity of television news depends less on the fixed attributes of viewers, such as their level of education, than on qualities that change with changing circumstances such as their partisanship, interest, and activism. Partisanship depends, in some small measure at least, upon the success enjoyed by the incumbent administration, on the policies the parties adopt, and on the appeal of the candidates the parties nominate (this evidence is summarized in Kinder and Sears 1985). Similarly, interest and activism depend partly on circumstances, rising in response to strong provocations and ample opportunities, declining as provocations fade and opportunities close (Hansen and Rosenstone 1984). Thus the capacity of television news to set the public's agenda waxes and wanes with changes in politics. Events that weaken partisanship, interest, and participation reduce the resources the public could otherwise draw upon to resist television news influence. By the same token, events that strengthen partisanship, interest, and participation thereby produce a more resourceful viewing public, one less likely to be buffeted about by the sketches of national life presented each night by the evening news.

The Priming Effect

The preceding chapters have supported the agenda-setting claim lavishly: television news does indeed influence the priorities the American public assigns to national problems. But the power of the networks does not end with viewers' political agendas. Beginning here, we take up the more subtle and more consequential possibility of what we will call priming. *By calling attention to some matters while ignoring others, television news influences the standards by which governments, presidents, policies, and candidates for public office are judged.*

Priming refers to changes in the standards that people use to make political evaluations. In assessing the performance of a government, a president, a policy, or a candidate, citizens can apply any number of standards. Our view of President Reagan, for example, might be influenced by his stance on arms control, the vitality of the national economy, his position on abortion, his judicial appointments, his performances at press conferences, and much, much more. According to the priming hypothesis, should television news become preoccupied with, say, the prospects of nuclear annihilation, then citizens would judge the president primarily by his success, as they see it, in reducing the risk of war. Should television news shift its attention to the economy citizens would follow suit, now evaluating the president largely by his success, as they see it, in maintaining prosperity—at least according to the priming hypothesis.

Our main business in this chapter is to see whether there is anything to such claims. We develop a theory of priming, argue for its psychological plausibility, and then test it against a series of television experiments focusing on presidential performance.[1]

A THEORY OF PRIMING

For theoretical guidance we have drawn upon ideas developed within the information processing perspective in psychology. Our general point of departure is Simon's observation that "human thinking powers are very modest when compared with the complexities of the environments in which human beings live. Faced with complexity and uncer-

tainty, lacking the wits to optimize, they must be content to satisfice—
to find 'good enough' solutions to their problems and 'good enough'
courses of action" (1979, 3). Like Simon, we find it useful to begin with
the modest assumptions about human cognitive capacity typically made
in psychological theory and corroborated in psychological research.

A major conclusion of such research is that people do not pay attention to everything. To do so would breed paralysis. Attention is highly
selective; people notice only particular features of special consequence.
Because of this fundamental limitation, the impressions we form of
others tend to be organized around a few central themes (Asch 1946).
With respect to the impressions we form of presidents, such themes
might include the political party he represents, the policies he favors
or opposes, his performance in office—the achievements and failures
he has appeared to bring about, the kind of person he seems to be,
particularly with respect to his apparent competence and integrity, the
racial, religious, class and ethnic groups he stands for and against, and
the general values he appears to embrace. These themes represent the
central standards against which presidents are measured.

A second conclusion of research on judgment is that rather than
undertaking exhaustive analysis, people ordinarily prefer heuristics—
intuitive shortcuts and simple rules of thumb. One such heuristic is
reliance upon information that is most *accessible*. When asked to
evaluate a particular president, Americans do not consider everything
they know. Nor do they even consider everything they know relevant
to the central themes listed above. Instead, they draw upon a sample of
what they know, and a sample of convenience at that. Some considerations prove decisive; others are ignored altogether. The relative importance of each depends in part on its momentary accessibility. Fischhoff,
Slovic, and Lichtenstein put the general point well: "People solve
problems, including the determination of their own values, with what
comes to mind. The more detailed, exacting, and creative their inferential process, the more likely they are to think of all they know
about the problem. The briefer that process becomes, the more they
will be controlled by the relative accessibility of various considerations" (1980, 127). Under ordinary circumstances, judgments about the
president are offered rather casually. Because the judgment process is
seldom "detailed, exacting, and creative," judgments of the president
depend less on the entire repertoire of people's knowledge and more
on which aspects of their knowledge happen to come to mind.

The importance of accessibility as a heuristic device in everyday
judgment is supported by considerable experimental evidence. Consider these examples: (1) Americans are more likely to say that they pay
a fair share of federal income tax if they have just been asked a battery

of questions probing their support for popular programs like aid to education and environmental protection than if they have not (Turner and Krauss 1978). Presumably, questions about particular and popular uses of tax monies primed people to take such uses into account when they decided whether their own tax burden was fair; (2) Americans report themselves to be substantially less interested in politics if they are first reminded of their limited political knowledge by being taken through a series of difficult questions regarding the activities of their representative in Washington, than if they are asked about their interest before this series of questions (Bishop, Oldendick, and Tuchfarber 1982); (3) More generally, Kahneman and Tversky have demonstrated that sizable shifts in choice can be produced by "seemingly inconsequential changes in the formulation of choice problems" (Tversky and Kahneman 1981, 453; also see Kahneman and Tversky 1979, 1984). Framing the problem in one way rather than in a logically equivalent alternative way can radically alter which options are chosen and which foregone.[2]

The upshot of all this research is not that judgment in general or political judgment in particular is capricious. Indeed, Kahneman and Tversky offer their own prospect theory as a systematic alternative to the conventional theory of rational choice they attack. The point is rather that a person's judgment depends in part on what comes to mind—on considerations that are, for whatever reason and however briefly, accessible.[3]

To a considerable degree, what information is accessible for presidential evaluations and what is not is a matter of circumstance. When political circumstances change, what comes to the citizen's mind most readily will also change. The circumstantial basis for judgments of presidential performance no doubt has many sources, but among the most important may be television news. We suggest that the standards citizens use to judge a president may be substantially determined by which stories newscasts choose to cover and, consequently, which considerations are made generally accessible. The more attention television news pays to a particular problem—the more frequently a problem area is primed—the more viewers should incorporate what they know about that problem into their overall judgment of the president.

EXPERIMENTAL TESTS OF PRIMING

SEQUENTIAL EXPERIMENTS

Although designed primarily to test the agenda-setting hypothesis, experiments 1, 2, and 9 also provide evidence relevant to priming. All three experiments followed the standard sequential procedure. In ex-

periment 1, participants viewed newscasts that either emphasized inadequacies in U.S. defense preparedness or did not; in experiment 2,
one group of participants watched newscasts emphasizing defense,
while another watched newscasts dotted with stories about inflation;[4]
in experiment 9, participants either viewed newscasts that paid special
attention to unemployment or did not.

We are interested in whether such experimentally-induced variations in news coverage influenced the standards viewers applied in
evaluating the president's overall performance. With this purpose in
mind, we asked participants on the final day of each experiment
(twenty-four hours after the last broadcast) to rate the president's performance with regard to various problems, including "maintaining a
strong defense" (experiments 1 and 2), "reducing inflation" (experiment
2), and "keeping unemployment down" (experiment 9). Participants
were also requested to evaluate the president's general performance.[5]

If the priming hypothesis is correct, we should find that viewers
who were shown stories about a particular problem gave more weight
to the president's performance *on that problem* when evaluating the
president's overall performance. In experiment 1, for example, people
who were exposed to a steady stream of stories about defense should
weigh defense performance more heavily in their evaluation of Carter's
overall performance than should people whose attention was directed
elsewhere. Put more formally, we estimate priming as the difference
between the impact of ratings of the president's handling of a particular
problem on evaluations of the president's general performance when
television news covers the problem and when it does not. (Details on
estimation are provided in Appendix B.)

The results from experiments 1, 2, and 9, displayed together in
table 7.1, support the priming hypothesis forcefully.[6] Consider, for example, the findings from experiment 1. Among participants in experiment 1 whose newscasts contained no stories about defense, a one
point improvement in ratings of Carter's handling of defense (between
fair and good, for example) was associated with about a one-quarter
point (.27: the baseline condition) improvement in evaluations of his
general job performance. Among viewers exposed to defense stories,
in contrast, the impact of ratings of the president's performance on defense was more than twice as great. For viewers who were primed
with defense, a one point improvement in their assessment of Carter's
performance on defense produced nearly a two-thirds of a point improvement in their evaluations of his general job performance (.62: the
primed condition).

Priming was just as substantial for defense and inflation in experiment 2. It was notably less for employment in experiment 9, no doubt because concern over unemployment was pervasive even without any experimental intervention. Note that the baseline coefficient in experiment 9 was .69, by far the largest we encountered in all our experiments. Experiment 9, remember, was conducted in July of 1982, during the depths of a serious recession. At this time, unemployment already dominated the public's political calculus. Even so, exposure to still more news about unemployment in experiment 9 did enhance, if marginally, the importance of unemployment in citizens' views of Mr. Reagan's overall performance as president.

In some ways, the results from the three experiments are unexpectedly strong. Experiments 1, 2, and 9 were designed with agenda-setting in mind, not priming. For the purpose of testing the priming hypothesis, they included too few participants in each condition, they omitted questions asking participants to evaluate the president's performance on the preexperimental questionnaire (which would have permitted a more sensitive test of priming), and they ignored subtle features of the newscasts that might well influence the magnitude of priming (such as implications regarding the president's responsibilities for causing or solving the problem). Despite these limitations—in fact, *because* of them—we take these results to be strong, if preliminary, support for priming.

Experiment 8 was designed to overcome these limitations and so to test priming in a particularly powerful way. Residents of the greater New Haven community were recruited in the usual manner and ran-

TABLE 7.1

Priming Presidential Evaluations: The Impact of Problem Performance Ratings on Evaluations of Presidential Performance as a Function of TV News Coverage (ordinary least squares estimates)

Experiment	Problem	No TV Coverage (Baseline)	TV Coverage (Primed)	Difference: Primed Minus Baseline
1	Defense	.27	.62	.35***
2	Defense	.26	.72	.46***
2	Inflation	−.01	.37	.38**
9	Unemployment	.69	.73	.04*

$*p < .25$
$**p < .05$
$***p < .01$

domly assigned to one of three treatments. One group of people
viewed newscasts over the course of a week emphasizing unemployment (three stories, for a total of ten minutes). A second group saw
newscasts emphasizing arms control (three stories, nine minutes in
total). A third group saw newscasts featuring steady coverage of civil
rights (three stories, seven minutes total). In the postexperimental
questionnaire, all participants rated Reagan's performance with regard
to unemployment, the nuclear arms race, and civil rights, and also
evaluated Reagan's overall performance as president.

In creating newscasts for experiment 8, we selected stories that implied a high degree of presidential responsibility: stories that suggested the president to be responsible either for causing a particular
problem or for solving it. Our assumption was that priming should be
most pronounced when the president was so implicated. We develop
this assumption further and test it in chapter 9. Here we merely assume that the level of presidential responsibility conveyed in television
coverage influences the magnitude of priming, so we did our best in
experiment 8 to hold presidential responsibility at a uniformly high
level in all three treatments.[7]

As in experiments 1, 2, and 9, we test priming by examining the
effect of the viewers' ratings of the president's performance on *particular* problems on their assessment of his *general* performance. This
may depend upon the prominence accorded those problems by television news. The results, shown in table 7.2, indicate strong support
for priming. The estimated effects due to priming shown there are
sizable, for arms control, civil rights, and unemployment alike. In each
of the three cases, the importance of the particular problem for the
president's overall standing more than *doubled*, thanks only to increases in television news coverage.[8] Together with the earlier analyses

TABLE 7.2

Priming Presidential Evaluations: The Impact of Problem Performance Ratings on
Evaluations of Presidential Performance as a Function of TV News Coverage:
Experiment 8 (ordinary least squares estimates)

Problem	No TV Coverage (Baseline)	TV Coverage (Primed)	Difference: Primed Minus Baseline
Arms control	.03	.49	.46*
Civil rights	.24	.68	.44*
Unemployment	.37	.83	.46*

*$p < .01$

of experiments 1, 2, and 9, these results demonstrate that television news powerfully shapes the standards viewers use to evaluate the president.

ASSEMBLAGE EXPERIMENTS

Partly to investigate the relationship between the intensity of news coverage and the magnitude of priming, we undertook two assemblage experiments. In experiments 3 and 4, participants viewed a collection of news stories at a single one hour sitting. Experiment 3 was run in April and May of 1981 with Yale University undergraduates and included five experimental conditions. Students saw either *no* stories about energy problems, *three* stories on energy, or *six* energy stories scattered through the collection; and such stories implied either *strong* presidential responsibility for the nation's energy predicament or *moderate* responsibility. Experiment 4 was conducted during June and July of 1981, with participants drawn from the general New Haven community. As in experiment 3, two levels of coverage (three stories vs. six stories) were combined with two degrees of presidential responsibility (strong vs. moderate), this time for each of three problems: energy, defense, and inflation. Thus participants saw either three stories or six stories about the target problem, and such stories pointed responsibility either toward or away from the president. In both experiments, after watching the collection of news stories, participants rated Carter's success in a variety of specific areas, including "implementing a national energy policy" (experiments 3 and 4), "holding inflation in check" (experiment 4), and "maintaining a strong national defense" (experiment 4), and also evaluated Carter's general performance as president.

Experiments 3 and 4 were obviously designed to investigate how, if at all, the degree of presidential responsibility implicit in television news coverage contributes to the priming effect. We will find out, but not until chapter 9. For now, we ignore the level of presidential responsibility and concentrate on the more elementary relationship between the magnitude of priming and the sheer amount of coverage. Therefore we test for priming effects in experiments 3 and 4 exactly as we did in the sequential experiments (see Appendix B for details).

The results from both experiments, displayed together in table 7.3, reveal consistent and substantial support for priming. In experiment 3, energy performance ratings were more influential in evaluations of Mr. Carter's general performance among students exposed to stories about energy than among those exposed to no stories about energy. The identical pattern appeared in experiment 4 for energy, defense, and infla-

TABLE 7.3

Priming Presidential Evaluations: The Impact of Problem Performance Ratings on
Evaluations of Overall Presidential Performance as a Function of TV News Coverage
(ordinary least squares estimates)

Experiment	Problem	No TV Coverage (Baseline)	TV Coverage (Primed)	Difference: Primed Minus Baseline
3	Energy	.18	.25	.07**
4	Energy	.19	.33	.14**
4	Defense	.04	.12	.08*
4	Inflation	.25	.39	.14**

*p < .20
**p < .05

tion alike. Although these priming effects are generally smaller than
those recorded in sequential experiments—as well they should be—
they nevertheless provide additional and clear support to the priming
hypothesis.[9]

TESTING AN ALTERNATIVE TO PRIMING

According to both sequential and assemblage experiments, when television news increases its coverage of a particular problem, viewers
weigh their ratings of the president's performance on that problem
more heavily when they evaluate the president's general performance.
This result is, of course, what we have termed priming—problems
covered by television news become more accessible and therefore
more important in the viewer's political calculus. However, the result is
consistent with an alternative view: that television coverage of a particular problem causes viewers to adjust their ratings of the president's
performance on that problem to become consistent with their overall
evaluation of the president. This possibility, which is the very opposite
of priming, we call *projection*.

How might projection work? Suppose the networks run a series of
stories on unemployment. Such stories supply viewers with new information and may remind them of what they already know. In evaluating
the new information and mulling over the old, people are very likely,
in part, to be guided by their prior opinions. In particular, the president's supporters and his critics may interpret the television stories
quite differently. His supporters may take the news about unemployment as indicating that things are not so bad; that they're getting better,

and in any case, that high unemployment is caused not by the president's policies, but by foreign competition or by the failed policies of the past. The president's critics, on the other hand, may see things as bad and getting worse, and may hold him directly accountable. The result of such ruminations will be that viewers' ratings of the president's performance on unemployment will now closely reflect their overall evaluation of him—not because unemployment dominates their overall impression, but because they have projected their overall impression onto the president's unemployment performance. What we have termed priming may in fact be projection.

Not only is projection a plausible alternative interpretation, it is an alternative with real consequence. The political differences between priming and projection are enormous. If priming holds, then television news possesses the capacity to alter the standards by which a president is judged, and therefore the degree of public popularity a president enjoys and the power he can wield. If projection holds, then we will have discovered that people interpret new events or reinterpret old events in order to maintain consistency with their existing predispositions—an interesting discovery, though hardly a new one (e.g., Abelson 1959) and, most important, one that implies a sharply reduced role for television news as a molder of opinion.

Disentangling priming from projection requires a departure from standard statistical procedures. In estimating priming effects so far, we have assumed that overall evaluations have no impact on specific performance ratings. If this is mistaken, which is the same as saying that projection is present, then our estimates of priming are positively biased. Obviously we need estimates of priming that are purged of projection. For this purpose, we turn again to experiment 8. An essential feature of that experiment was that participants were asked to evaluate President Reagan on two occasions, before and after watching the television broadcasts, six days apart. This enables us to obtain estimates of priming uncontaminated by projection.

To do so, we relied on the method of two stage least squares (2SLS) (see Appendix B for details). We followed this procedure for the three problems separately, each time estimating the impact of problem performance on overall evaluation for the experimental group and for the control group. If priming is at work, the 2SLS estimate of the impact of problem performance on overall performance should be greater when the problem is primed than when it is not. That is, priming is indicated by the *difference* between the two estimates: the impact of ratings of performance on the target problem on overall performance should be more pronounced among those who have just watched newscasts dotted with stories devoted to that problem, than among those whose newscasts were purged of such stories.

The results from this analysis support the priming hypothesis handsomely. Once projection is taken into account, priming effects persist. If anything, these results suggest that our earlier estimates of priming somewhat *understated* the impact of television news (see Appendix B for details).

CONCLUSIONS

By providing glimpses of some aspects of national life while neglecting others, television news helps define the standards that viewers apply to presidential performance. Our experiments show priming to be a robust effect; it occurs in coverage of various problems, for both Democratic and Republican presidents; in different experimental arrangements, and in analyses that remove the effects due to projection. Together, these results constitute impressive support for priming.

Although we detected priming in every experiment, the effects were more pronounced in sequential experiments than in assemblage experiments. On average, priming coefficients derived from experiments 1, 2, 8, and 9 were more than three times as great as those derived from experiments 3 and 4 (.37 vs. .11). This contrast is strongly reminiscent of the pattern of results we found with respect to agenda-setting in chapter 3. There, as here, periodic exposure spread over several days appeared to be more influential than a single concentrated exposure. The contrast is important, since the periodic exposure that is characteristic of sequential experiments represents more faithfully the ordinary citizen's actual encounters with television news than does the sudden burst of exposure that is the defining feature of assemblage experiments.[10]

The next several chapters probe more deeply into priming. We will see whether priming can be detected not only in viewers' assessments of the president's performance but also in assessments of his character (chapter 8); whether priming is strengthened when the news implies that the president or his administration is responsible for the problem (chapter 9); who among the viewing public is most susceptible to priming (chapter 10); and how, if at all, priming influences the considerations that voters take into account as they cast their ballots (chapter 11).

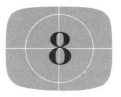

Priming and Presidential Character

From chapter 7 it is apparent that television coverage can effectively prime viewers' judgments of a president's performance. Now we determine the extent to which coverage can also prime viewers' judgments of a president's *character*. This is hardly a frivolous generalization. Presidential campaigns are many things: competitions between the two major political parties; ideological struggles over the direction of national policy; referenda on the incumbent's performance in office. But they are also tests of character (Kinder and Abelson 1981). Candidates must project intelligence, honesty, compassion and more, or suffer the consequences. More generally, how much support a president can muster during his term and how many votes he receives on election day depend heavily on how he is judged in personal terms. Because character is important to the public, it becomes important to our analysis of priming.

To test whether television news can prime the standards viewers apply to presidential character, we must first identify those aspects of a president's character that voters deem most important. In doing so, we have assumed, as Lane did, that "people seek in leaders the same qualities they seek in friends, that is, they simply generalize their demands from one case to the other" (1978, 447). According to four autonomous lines of research in psychology, such demands seem to center on the largely independent dimensions of *competence* and *sociability*. These two dimensions emerge as critical traits in investigations of leadership in small groups (task vs. socioemotional leadership, Cartwright and Zander 1968); in attitude change research on source credibility (expertise vs. trust, McGuire 1985); in research on interpersonal attraction (respect vs. affection, Rubin 1973); and, perhaps most pertinent here, in explorations of the criteria people apply in evaluating friends and acquaintances (intellectual competence vs. affection, Rosenberg 1977).

Americans also seem to demand competence and some version of sociability from their president, though the evidence to date is rather sketchy. References to competence and sociability emerge frequently in voters' open-ended commentaries on presidential candidates (Miller and Miller 1976; Page 1978). Moreover, structural analysis of trait inventories developed with the purpose of identifying core aspects of presidential character generally reveal two correlated but distinct dimensions that are strongly reminiscent of the results from psychology. One dimension we call *competence*, represented best by specific traits like "experienced" and "knowledgeable"; the other we call *integrity*, represented by such traits as "moral" and "honest" (Kinder and Abelson 1981; Kinder 1985).

One set of results illustrating this point is presented in table 8.1. Nationally representative samples of Americans of voting age interviewed by the Center for Political Studies during the 1980 presidential election season were asked how well each of seven character traits described Jimmy Carter, and, in a separate series of questions, Ronald Reagan.[1] Four of these traits—"knowledgeable," "inspiring," "weak," and "provides strong leadership"—were meant to represent competence; the remaining three—"moral," "dishonest," and "power-hungry"—were intended to represent integrity. A factor analysis of respondents' answers to these questions, shown in table 8.1, indicates that their character assessments of Carter and Reagan are indeed organized around the themes of competence and integrity. (See Appendix B for technical details on the factor analysis.) Although naturally correlated—for example, Americans who regarded the president as competent also tended to think of him as a man of high integrity—the two themes are conceptually separate and empirically distinct.

TABLE 8.1

Factor Analysis of Candidate Traits: Factor Loadings

	Carter		Reagan	
	Competence	Integrity	Competence	Integrity
Knowledgeable	.61	.03	.65	−.02
Inspiring	.78	−.05	.76	−.00
Weak	−.51	−.19	−.18	−.36
Strong Leader	.86	−.04	.72	.11
Moral	.19	.41	.36	.36
Dishonest	.12	−.81	.09	−.74
Power-hungry	−.09	−.48	−.10	−.49
Correlation between competence factor and integrity factor		.50		.59

Source: 1980 National Election Study

Distinctions between general performance, competence, and integrity are worth making here, since television news coverage that is influential for one may be irrelevant for another. We anticipate the largest priming effects on judgments of a president's general performance, because viewers' judgments of overall performance are presumably some average sense of how well they see the president managing unemployment, foreign relations, and other pressing national problems. Priming viewers with news about one such problem naturally enhances the importance they assign to it in judging how well the president is performing overall.

Judgments of competence should also be influenced, but not as much, because coverage of national problems and judgments of competence are not quite so entangled in viewers' minds. A president who presides over a declining unemployment rate will no doubt point to this achievement as evidence of his competence. But many viewers will recognize that performance in any particular domain reflects the president's knowledge and leadership skills imperfectly. Performance in any problem area is always determined in part by forces beyond even the most capable president's control. In the case of unemployment, for example, Congress, corporations, unions, the international economy, and more all come into play. As a consequence, television coverage is more likely to activate information relevant to viewers' judgments of the president's overall performance than it is information relevant to judgments of his personal competence.

Following this logic further, we expect priming effects to be faintest for judgments of the president's integrity. We assume that *citizens* assume that the state of national problems like unemployment or rising prices—the focus of our experimental variations—have little to do with the president's personal integrity. If this is correct, then judgments of the president's integrity should be little-influenced by our experimental manipulations of television coverage.[2]

ANALYSIS AND RESULTS

We tested this general expectation of graded priming effects—that we would see the greatest impact on judgments of the president's overall performance, an intermediate impact on judgments of the president's competence, and a weak if not negligible impact on judgments of the president's integrity—by returning to the six experiments described in chapter 7. In each, participants not only evaluated the president's overall performance, but also judged how well the president could be described by a set of character traits. In experiment 1, for example, the specific traits were smart, weak, knowledgeable, immoral, power-hungry, and dishonest. The first three reflect the general theme of competence; the second three reflect integrity. Across the six experiments, there was some variation in the length and format of the trait battery and in its specific elements, but competence and integrity were always represented (and always by at least three items). In each case, we averaged replies to the competence items to form a competence index and did the same with replies to the integrity items to form an integrity index.[3]

To determine the extent to which television news coverage primed judgments of presidential character, we simply reestimated the various priming effects reported in chapter 7, replacing evaluations of the president's general performance first with assessments of his competence and then with assessments of the president's integrity. If the priming gradient holds, priming effects should diminish as we move from general performance to competence to integrity.

Figure 8.1 displays the relevant findings from the two assemblage experiments (3 and 4), while figure 8.2 does the same for the four sequential experiments (1, 2, 8, and 9). For purposes of examining the full priming gradient, both figures include the priming effects associated with general performance as well, taken from chapter 7.

Results from the two assemblage experiments conform neatly to the

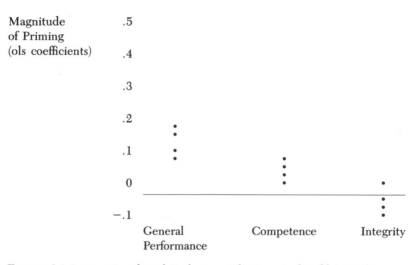

FIGURE 8.1 Priming Presidential Evaluations: The Impact of Problem Performance Ratings on Evaluations of Presidential Performance, Competence, and Integrity as a Function of TV News Coverage: Experiments 3 and 4 (ordinary least squares estimates)

expected pattern (see figure 8.1). For evaluations of President Carter's overall performance, all four priming effects were statistically significant, averaging .11. Priming effects associated with assessments of President Carter's competence were noticeably smaller. They averaged .05; three of the four effects approached but did not quite attain statistical significance ($.15 < p < .25$). Finally, priming effects diminished still further in assessments of President Carter's integrity. As shown in the last column of figure 8.1, three of the four estimated priming effects were in fact negative; none was reliably different from zero ($p > .25$); the average effect was $-.03$. Thus in these two experiments, priming was most pronounced in evaluations of the president's general performance, only modest in evaluations of his competence, and nonexistent in judgments of his integrity, just as we had anticipated.

The findings are murkier and, depending on one's tastes, more interesting, in the four sequential experiments (see figure 8.2). These results do support the gradient hypothesis in one respect, since priming effects were generally more pronounced when viewers were asked to evaluate the president's overall performance than when they were asked to evaluate his character. Contrary to the gradient hypothesis, however, priming was often stronger in judgments of the president's integrity than in judgments of his competence. A closer look reveals that this reversal is confined entirely to judgments of President Reagan. In

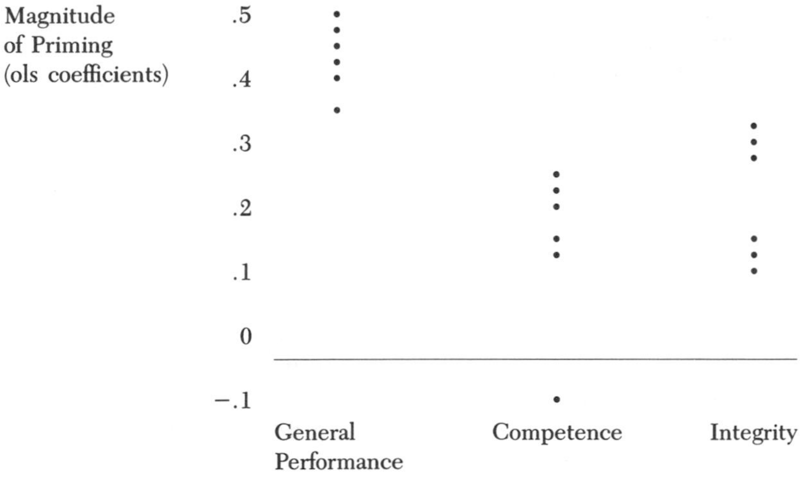

FIGURE 8.2 Priming Presidential Evaluations: The Impact of Problem Performance Ratings on Evaluations of Presidential Performance, Competence, and Integrity as a Function of TV News Coverage: Experiments 1, 2, 8, and 9 (ordinary least squares estimates)

experiments 8 and 9, President Reagan was the target, and in *none* of
the four tests did the expected pattern emerge. For President Reagan,
the average priming effect was .18 for competence and .34 for integrity. Why were judgments of Mr. Reagan's integrity primed so
powerfully?

We can pursue this puzzle further while at the same time providing
additional tests of the gradient hypothesis by making use of the 1980
and 1982 National Election Studies. The 1980 National Election Study
consists of two parts: personal interviews with a national cross-section
of Americans of voting age conducted in September and October of
1980, as the presidential election reached its climax; and personal interviews in September of 1980 with a national panel of Americans of
voting age that had already been interviewed twice before, once just
prior to the New Hampshire Primary, and once in June, immediately
after the last set of primary elections. In both the cross-section and
panel interviews, respondents were asked to rate President Carter's
performance in five specific domains: inflation, energy, unemployment, the Iranian Hostage Crisis, and the Soviet Union's invasion of
Afghanistan.[4] Respondents also were requested to provide general assessments of President Carter: his overall performance as president,
his competence, and his integrity.[5] By making separate use of the September–October cross-section and the September wave of the panel
survey, we can provide two concurrent yet independent tests of the
gradient hypothesis with President Carter as the target of evaluation.

Results from both the cross-section and panel surveys, summarized
in table 8.2, support the gradient hypothesis in every detail (see Appendix B for details on estimation). According to these findings, citizens' general evaluations of President Carter during the fall of 1980
were dominated by their assessments of his handling of inflation, and
to a lesser extent, by their ratings of his management of the nation's
energy predicament and the Iranian hostage crisis. As the gradient hypothesis predicts, the impact of these performance ratings was greatest
for assessments of President Carter's general performance, was apparent though much less striking for assessments of his competence, and
virtually disappeared for assessments of his integrity.

Thus these survey results, based on two independent samples and
two quite different analyses (one of which controls for projection effects), strongly corroborate our experimental findings. The gradient
hypothesis stands up very well to a variety of tests—at least where
President Carter is concerned.

President Reagan is another matter. In the 1982 National Election
Study, conducted in the aftermath of the midterm House elections, a

TABLE 8.2

Estimated Impact of Problem Performance Ratings on Overall Evaluations of
President Carter

Problem	Evaluation of President Carter's:		
	General Performance	Competence	Integrity
September–October 1980[†]			
Inflation	.45**	.20**	.10*
Energy	.16**	.12**	.07
Unemployment	.10*	.08*	.06
Hostage crisis	.18**	.10*	.08*
Afghanistan	.04	.03	.03
Number of cases	1387	1386	1375
September 1980[††]			
Inflation	.50**	.29**	.17*
Energy	.33**	.13*	.04
Unemployment	−.09	−.09	−.06
Hostage crisis	−.09	−.03	−.01
Afghanistan	.06	−.04	−.01
Number of cases	634	624	624

*$p < .10$

**$p < .01$

[†] Source: 1980 National Election Study Cross Section (ordinary least squares estimates)

[††] Source: 1980 National Election Study Panel (two-stage least squares estimates)

representative sample of Americans of voting age was asked to rate
Mr. Reagan's performance in a variety of specific domains—most notably on arms control, unemployment, national defense, and inflation—
as well as to assess his general performance as president, his competence, and his integrity.[6] Table 8.3 shows the impact of the specific
ratings on the general assessments. The results displayed there indicate that inflation dominated the public's evaluations of President
Reagan, just as it did two years earlier in evaluations of Carter.[7] And as
held true for Carter, ratings of Reagan's performance on inflation affected assessments of his general performance more than they affected
assessments of his character. In these respects, the results are perfectly
consistent with the gradient hypothesis. Contrary to the gradient hypothesis, however, ratings of President Reagan's performance on inflation mattered somewhat more to Americans' views of his integrity
(priming coefficient = .21) than to their views of his competence (priming coefficient = .16). This survey result contravenes the gradient hypothesis, and in exactly the same way as did our experimental results on
Reagan. Evidently something is amiss with the gradient hypothesis.[8]

TABLE 8.3

Estimated Impact of Problem Performance Ratings on Overall Evaluations of
President Reagan: November–December 1982 (ordinary least squares estimates)

Problem	Evaluation of President Reagan's:		
	General Performance	Competence	Integrity
Arms control	.08	.08	.06
Unemployment	.21	.09	.07
Defense	.11	.09	.08
Inflation	.44	.16	.21
Number of cases	877	907	899

Source: 1982 National Election Study
Note: All coefficients are statistically significant $p < .01$.

Conclusions

According to the results presented in this chapter, television news influences not only the standards viewers apply to presidential performance, but the standards they apply to presidential character as well. As we had expected, priming was consistently more powerful in judgments of presidential performance than in judgments of presidential character. Nevertheless, the results leave little doubt that the public's view of the president's personal qualities depends on which aspects of national life television news chooses to cover and which to ignore. The terms of character are set, in part, by television news, just as the terms of performance are.

We had also expected that priming would be more pronounced in viewers' judgments of the president's competence than in judgments of his integrity. This expectation held only for President Carter; contrary to our expectations, priming effects were generally more apparent in viewers' judgments of President Reagan's integrity than in judgments of his competence. This reversal of the anticipated result—in both experimental and survey tests—suggests that the simple and straightforward gradient hypothesis must be revised, if not abandoned altogether.

The gradient hypothesis presumes that viewers work out the implications of news stories in a reasonably logical way. Thus coverage of unemployment has implications for the president's competence but not for the president's integrity. Such simple and straightforward logic does not seem to correspond to the way our viewers actually behaved. Our results suggest an alternative process.

It may be that news media in general and network news in particular tend to frame stories about the president in ways that center on weakness or controversy. In 1980, television was overflowing with stories that questioned not whether President Carter was a decent fellow (integrity), but whether he was up to his job (competence). In 1982, in the wake of Reagan's stunning legislative successes, the burning question was not whether Reagan could govern (competence), but whether his programs were fair and whether he cared for the poor (a variation on the integrity theme). During the Carter years, events were generally construed by the press and interpreted by the public as signs of the president's competence—or lack thereof. During the Reagan years, events were generally construed by the press and understood by the public as signs of the president's compassion—or lack thereof. Problematic aspects of the president's character capture the media's attention and therefore, perhaps, become central traits for the public.

This is, of course, mere speculation on our part. The argument fits our results, but this is not much of an achievement, since we devised the argument to do just that. Slightly more persuasively, it is also generally consistent with results reported by others. It turns out that the relative importance voters attach to competence and integrity varies sharply from one context to the next. Partly this has to do with the special qualities of candidates, which, we assume, attract special attention from the media. For example, George McGovern's campaign fiascoes in the 1972 presidential contest commanded massive coverage and comment. Meanwhile, and unremarkably, voters seemed preoccupied with the Democratic candidate's competence. One analysis of the 1972 campaign argues persuasively that McGovern's eventual downfall had much to do with his apparent inability to manage a campaign (Popkin, Gorman, Phillips, and Smith 1976). Another example, just as dramatic but with the emphasis on integrity, is provided by Edward Kennedy. Apparently by virtue of his distinctive personal history, for Kennedy alone among a set of 1980 presidential contenders, judgments of integrity were more consequential in determining preference than were considerations of competence (Kinder and Abelson 1981).

More generally, the tenor of the times may also contribute to the relative importance voters attach to competence and integrity in presidential assessments (Barber 1980; Page 1978). The "long national nightmare" of Watergate may well have enhanced the importance of integrity in the 1976 campaign and may therefore have contributed to the success of Jimmy Carter's candidacy, with its unrelenting emphasis upon decency and trust. Conversely, the domestic and international difficulties faced by the Carter administration helped make competence a central question in 1980. This is priming on a huge scale, with possibly huge political consequences.

Priming and Presidential Responsibility

To this point we have shown that television news rearranges the standards by which viewers assess a president's performance and character. Here we examine whether such priming effects depend on how news stories are framed. In particular, we will see whether priming depends upon the prominence of the president in the news: is priming strengthened when television news encourages viewers to attach responsibility to the president?

ASSIGNING RESPONSIBILITY FOR NATIONAL PROBLEMS

Was President Carter perpetrator or victim of double-digit inflation? Was the 1982 recession brought on by President Reagan's policies or by the policies of his predecessors? These are difficult questions, and in attempting to answer them the public may be influenced by television news stories, which vary sharply in the degree to which they imply a president's responsibilities. For example, a story on rising food prices might refer to a persistent drought as the probable cause—or might suggest instead that prices are rising because the president's farm policies discourage cultivation. Such differences are likely to be consequential. We suggest that *the more television coverage interprets events as though they were the result of the president's actions, the more influential such coverage will be in priming the public's assessment of the president's performance.*

Our reasoning here is drawn from attribution theory in social psychology. Attribution theory aspires to provide a systematic account of how ordinary people explain the mundane puzzles they encounter in everyday life. "If a person is aggressively competitive in his behavior, is he this kind of person, or is he reacting to situational pressures? . . . If a person fails on a test, does he have low ability, or is the test difficult?" (Kelley 1973, 107). Political thinking is full of comparable causal puzzles. If the national economy begins to sputter, for example, is it the president's doing, or are the causes to be found elsewhere—in Congress, corporations, unions, OPEC, or the American consumer?

Under circumstances of limited information, would-be attributors answer such questions first by drawing upon assumptions about what classes of causal forces, in what combination, could have produced the observed effect. According to Kelley, "the mature individual has a repertoire of such abstract ideas about the operation and interaction of causal factors. These conceptions enable him to make economical and fast attributional analysis, by providing a framework within which bits and pieces of relevant information can be fitted in order to draw reasonably good causal inferences" (1972, 2).

The simplest of these conceptions is multiple sufficiency: the assumption that an observed effect could have been produced by *either* of several plausible causes. Under this assumption, the role of any particular cause in producing an observed effect will be discounted if other plausible causes are also present. So, for example, Americans will be less apt to blame the president for inflation if: (1) they regard OPEC demands for huge increases in oil prices as an alternative plausible cause of inflation; and (2) such demands are given conspicuous treatment in the nation's media. In fact, Hibbs, Rivers, and Vasilatos reported evidence consistent with this claim in their analysis of public support for American presidents. They concluded that "the performance evaluation standards used by the public may be quite sophisticated in the sense that political leaders are not punished [or are punished less] for unfavorable economic disturbances outside their control" (1982a, 443). By the same logic, presidents should be punished more (priming should be augmented) when television news portrays national difficulties as if they were the president's doing.

In the remainder of this chapter, we describe the results of four assemblage experiments designed to examine the relationship between presidential responsibility and priming. In each we test the proposition, drawn from attribution theory, that priming is strengthened when television coverage focuses responsibility on the president and weakened when it shifts responsibility away from the president.[1]

RESPONSIBILITY AND PRIMING

As a preliminary investigation of the responsibility hypothesis, we undertook experiment 3 in April and May of 1981, using Yale University undergraduates as our subjects. Students were randomly assigned to one of five treatments. Participants viewed either no stories on energy, a few stories on energy, or many stories; and such stories either implied presidential responsibility for the nation's energy predicament or did not.[2] Experiment 4, a replication and extension of experiment 3, was completed during the summer of 1981. Once again, two levels of exposure were combined with two degrees of responsibility, this time for each of three problems: energy, defense, and inflation. Participants assigned to one of the four treatment conditions for a particular problem (e.g., defense) saw *no* stories about the other two problems (energy, inflation). In experiment 4 we resumed our normal practice of recruiting from the general New Haven community via classified advertisements placed in local newspapers.

The presentations for both experiments were assembled from news stories originally broadcast in 1979 and 1980. Participants assigned to high exposure conditions in either experiment saw six stories about the target problem sprinkled through the presentation, while participants assigned to low exposure conditions saw only three. In high responsibility presentations, stories in which the president (always Carter) was portrayed as responsible for a national problem outnumbered those stories that made no reference to the president by a margin of 2:1; in intermediate responsibility conditions, this ratio was reversed.[3]

We already know (from chapter 7) that both experiments 3 and 4 provided strong confirmation of the basic priming hypothesis. In experiment 3, energy performance ratings were more influential in evaluations of Mr. Carter's general performance among viewers exposed to stories about energy than among those exposed to no stories about energy. And so it was in experiment 4, for energy, defense, and inflation alike. Our first order of business here is to determine whether such effects are strengthened when coverage implies that the president is somehow responsible for the country's troubles. (As always, details on estimation can be found in Appendix B.)

The results from experiments 3 and 4 are displayed together in table 9.1. They indicate that viewers exposed to stories that portrayed the president as responsible for a problem did indeed take special account of the president's performance on that problem in evaluating his performance overall. As shown in table 9.1, in each of the four comparisons, conditions that emphasized the president's role led to greater priming. In experiment 3, for example, the president's performance on energy was roughly twice as important in determining his overall performance ratings among those shown energy stories that featured the president, than among those shown energy stories that did not. In the first instance, an improvement of one point in ratings of the president's success on the energy problem (from fair to good, for example) would be associated with a .38 improvement in ratings of the president's overall performance; in the latter, the same one point difference would produce just a .18 gain. On average, across the four comparisons, high presidential responsibility conditions enhanced the priming effect by about two-thirds. These appear to be sizable effects, but as reported in the last column of table 9.1, we cannot be certain that they are real. Altogether, then, the results are not as decisive as we had hoped. Everywhere we looked we turned up evidence consistent with the responsibility hypothesis, but nowhere was the evidence unequivocal.

To resolve this uncertainty, and to provide a more stringent test of the responsibility hypothesis, we conducted experiments 12 and 13. Perhaps experiments 3 and 4 proved indecisive because our manipulations of presidential responsibility were indecisive to begin with. In experiments 3 and 4, remember, the crucial comparison was between those who saw stories that mainly emphasized presidential responsibility (by a ratio of 2:1) and those who saw stories that mainly did not emphasize presidential responsibility (by the same 2:1 ratio). Thus *all* viewers saw some stories portraying the president's duties and obligations. In retrospect, differences between the high and intermediate responsibility conditions seem quite subtle; that they lead to discernible, if not quite unequivocal, differences in priming seems the more impressive.

Experiments 12 and 13, conducted in the spring and summer of 1983, provide a more powerful and symmetric test of the responsibility hypothesis. In experiment 12, participants drawn from the Ann Arbor community viewed a collection of news stories. Each included one story about either energy shortages or unemployment. Moreover, the story implied either that the president was responsible *both* for causing the problem and for curing it (the augmentation condition), or that forces and agents *other* than the president were responsible for the

TABLE 9.1

Priming Presidential Evaluation: The Impact of Problem Performance Ratings on Evaluations of the President's Performance as a Function of Presidential Responsibility in TV News Coverage (ordinary least squares estimates)

Experiment	Problem	TV Coverage Does *Not* Emphasize President	TV Coverage Does Emphasize President	Difference: High Minus Low Presidential Responsibility
3	Energy	.18	.38	.20**
4	Energy	.28	.46	.18***
4	Defense	.14	.32	.18**
4	Inflation	.42	.57	.15*

***$p < .4$
**$p < .5$
*$p < .6$

problem (the discounting condition), or was entirely *silent* on the matter of responsibility (the agnostic condition). We designed experiment 13 as a partial replication of experiment 12. This time residents of the Ann Arbor community were assigned to one of four viewing conditions (instead of six). Participants saw a collection of news stories that included a story either about energy shortages or unemployment. The story on energy shortages emphasized the president's responsibilities; the story on unemployment either emphasized the president's responsibilities, discounted his responsibilities, or was silent about them.

Experiments 12 and 13 thus manipulated presidential responsibility across a wide range—from newscasts that augment the president's role to newscasts that discount it. According to the responsibility hypothesis, priming should be weakest under discounting, intermediate in the agnostic conditions, and most pronounced under augmentation.[4]

The results, presented in table 9.2, confirm the hypothesis powerfully. When television coverage discounts the president's role, so, too, do viewers; when coverage augments the president's role, viewers do so as well. While the effects of responsibility are noticeable for both problems, they are especially conspicuous for energy. The impact of energy performance ratings on overall presidential performance evaluations almost quadrupled when the president's responsibilities were emphasized, over that when they were discounted (.49 vs. .13).

This difference between problems is reminiscent of a similar difference that emerged in experiments 3 and 4, where our manipulation of presidential responsibility strengthened priming most in the case of energy and least in the case of inflation. Perhaps these differences reflect the comparative novelty of national energy problems and familiarity of national economic difficulties. At least since Franklin Roose-

TABLE 9.2

Priming Presidential Evaluations: The Impact of Problem Performance Ratings on Evaluations of the President's Performance as a Function of Presidential Responsibility in TV News Coverage (ordinary least squares estimates)

| Experiment | Problem | TV News Treatment of President's Responsibilities | | | Difference: Augmented Minus Discounted |
		Discounted	Agnostic	Augmented	
12	Energy	.13	.31	.49	.36*
12	Unemployment	.29	.42	.55	.26**
13	Unemployment	.90	.94	.98	.08*

*$p < .3$
**$p < .2$

velt and the Great Depression, the American public has appeared to hold the president accountable for economic conditions. But who is to blame for energy shortages? And what institutions are responsible for seeing to it that such shortages do not recur? Because the answers in viewers' minds may be far less clear, those implied by the evening news may carry greater weight.

Of course, the major lesson of experiments 12 and 13, as well as of their two predecessors, is that priming depends not only on the sheer amount of coverage, but on its nature. When the news implies the president is responsible for causing and solving national problems, priming is strengthened; when the news discounts the president's role, priming is undermined.

RESPONSIBILITY AND UNCERTAINTY

Variations in presidential responsibility implied by the evening news may affect priming in an indirect way as well. It is not always obvious how well the president is performing in a particular domain. Whether or not the United States has an adequate defense is a most complex question. Nor is it easy for citizens to determine how much of U.S. defense preparedness is really the president's doing. News stories that portray the president as Commander-in-Chief invite the inference that the president is responsible for defense; stories that feature congressional cuts in defense or actions taken by U.S. allies may discourage viewers from either blaming or crediting the president. Consequently, what we have called augmentation coverage may be associated with greater viewer certainty about the president's performance (good or bad). Coverage that discounts the president's responsibilities, on the other hand, should breed viewer uncertainty as to how well the president is performing.

We tested this notion by examining the strength of viewers' opinions regarding the president's performance. Viewers should be more confident of how well the president is doing in a particular domain after seeing stories that emphasize his responsibilities, than after watching stories which imply that responsibility for the country's predicament rests elsewhere. Table 9.3 reports the proportion of people who said that they knew how the president was doing on energy, defense, inflation, and unemployment across different responsibility conditions for each of the four experiments. As indicated there, the predicted results show up for energy and energy alone. For defense, inflation, and unemployment, virtually all viewers under all conditions were quite will-

TABLE 9.3

Percentage of Viewers who Rated President's Performance on Specific Problems as a Function of the Level of Presidential Responsibility in TV News Coverage

Experiment	Problem	No TV Coverage	TV Coverage Emphasizes President's Responsibility	Difference: High Responsibility Minus No Coverage
3	Energy	81	100	19**
4	Energy	95	100	5*
4	Defense	94	96	2
4	Inflation	98	100	2
12	Energy	77	100	23***
12	Unemployment	97	100	3
13	Energy	72	95	23***
13	Unemployment	100	95	-5

$*p < .3$

$**p < .1$

$***p < .05$

ing to offer opinions on the president's performance. Viewers were generally less certain about the president's energy performance and, as expected, especially so after watching news stories about energy that ignored or discounted his role.

SUMMARY AND CONCLUSIONS

The influence of television news coverage on Americans' assessments of presidential performance depends partly on how the news portrays his responsibilities. As shown here, stories implying that the president is responsible for a national problem are more powerful in two respects: they lead viewers to greater certainty about his performance on that problem, and they induce viewers to attach greater importance to that performance in evaluating the president overall.

Both these effects appear to be stronger for problems that are relative newcomers to the American political agenda, for which the public's understanding is still in formation. Confronted with a problem like the energy crisis, citizens may be quite uncertain as to its causes and cures. More specifically, they may be unsure as to what part, if any, the president's policies have played in producing energy shortages, and what role the president can and should play in avoiding them in the future. Such conditions appear to open the way for greater priming effects. In the face of novelty and uncertainty, viewers may be substantially swayed by the way television news assigns responsibility.

The several experiments described in this chapter were inspired partly by attribution theory. Research on this topic in social psychology over the last decade has turned up a variety of errors that people commonly make in their everyday explanations. One such shortcoming is that people settle too readily on causes that are distinguished primarily by their momentary visibility and salience (Fiske and Taylor 1984). In the political realm no one is, of course, more visible than the president (Gans 1979; Grossman and Kumar 1981). And Americans do demand a great deal of their chief executive. Presidents are expected to provide prosperity, peace, order, justice, and more (Brody and Page 1975; Greenstein 1978). Attribution theory suggests that these two observations are connected. Partly because of the president's extraordinary visibility, the responsibilities assigned him may invariably surpass what any president can hope to achieve. Perhaps the fundamental attribution error in the realm of politics lies in the extravagant assumptions Americans make regarding what presidents can do—assumptions that, as we have seen here, may be promoted (if inadvertently) by television news.

Victims of Priming

According to the evidence already presented, television news shapes the standards by which the public evaluates the president—both his overall performance in office and the strengths and weaknesses of his character. In this chapter we try to identify characteristics of viewers that make them more or less susceptible to these effects. Who are the victims of priming?

As we did in a parallel analysis of agenda-setting in chapter 6, we look with particular interest here at education, partisanship, and political involvement. In chapter 6 we found that the capacity of television news to shape national priorities increased as viewers' political skills and interests declined. The farther away the viewer from the world of public affairs, the stronger the agenda-setting power of television news. Perhaps the same will hold for priming. Priming, too, may thrive among those with limited political resources: those with little formal education, no partisan attachments, indifferent to and unpracticed in the realm of politics.

Priming may also depend on the assumptions viewers make about presidential responsibility. As we've shown in chapter 9, news stories implying that the president is responsible for a national problem trigger priming more effectively than do stories implying that responsibility rests elsewhere. So priming is partly a matter of the degree to which the news connects a problem to the president. But priming may also depend on the degree to which *viewers* connect a problem to the president. That is, Americans may differ sharply from one another in what they take to be the president's obligations and responsibilities. The link between a particular national problem and the president's performance may be firmly in place in some viewers' minds, and missing altogether in others. Some see fluctuations in unemployment as primarily the president's doing; others would never consider such a possibility. We will refer to viewers' understanding of national problems as their "tacit theories." We suppose that viewers whose theories about a particular national problem include links to the president should be especially susceptible to priming.

ANALYSIS AND RESULTS

To explore who is more or less vulnerable to priming, we relied on three sequential experiments. Experiment 1 emphasized apparent inadequacies in American defense capability. Experiment 2 drew the viewer's attention either to the dilapidated condition of U.S. military forces and equipment, to the ravages of inflation, or to contamination of the natural environment. Finally, experiment 8 presented participants with news stories that either detailed cuts in job training programs implemented by the Reagan administration, documented Mr. Reagan's opposition to extending the 1965 Voting Rights Act, or featured his emphasis on military spending and reluctance to participate in arms control negotiations.[1]

Measures of education, partisanship, and involvement were included in all three experiments (the exact questions are given in chapter 6). Measures of viewers' tacit theories appeared only in experiment 8, however, and because they are new, we should say a word about them here. We presume in the first place that tacit theories consist partly of the *causes* people see for national problems. It is one thing to understand inflation as caused by avaricious oil sheikhs; quite another to locate the cause of rising prices in presidential malfeasance. Tacit theories also include assumptions about *moral accountability.* We presume that Americans are at least as much concerned about knowing *who* should solve the problems they see as they are about how problems arise. While causal assumptions are primarily bound up in the origin of problems, moral accountability attaches primarily to their solution. Agents and institutions are invested with moral accountability to the degree that they are seen as obliged to provide remedies. In order to measure tacit theories, then, we simply identified viewers who cited the president as among the principal causes of the current problem,[2] or who believed that responsibility for solving or ameliorating the problem lay partly if not entirely with the president.[3]

Our primary objective is to determine the extent to which priming is affected by the predispositions of the viewer. Does priming depend, as agenda-setting does, on just who is watching? In particular, is priming enhanced among those with little formal education? Among political independents? Among the apathetic and disengaged? Or among those whose tacit theories place the president at the center of national problems? Our analysis takes up each of these possibilities in turn, for each experiment and problem separately.

The results are shown in table 10.1. The coefficients displayed there

TABLE 10.1

Impact of Priming among Different Types of Viewers

Viewer Type	Experiment 1 Defense	Experiment 2 Defense	Experiment 2 Environment	Experiment 2 Inflation	Experiment 8 Arms Control	Experiment 8 Civil Rights	Experiment 8 Unemployment
Education							
High school or less	.24	-.21	.20	.45	.29*	-.11	-.18*
Party Identification							
Democrat	-.29	.01	.41**	-.09	-.41**	.23	.19*
Republican	.31	.26	-.43**	1.47**	.58***	-.67*	1.00
Involvement							
Follow public affairs rarely	.07	.11	.11	-.15	-.23**	.31*	-.01
Pays little attention to newspaper coverage of politics	.01	-.04	.01	-.09	.07	.04	-.08
Doesn't read a daily newspaper	.06	.37*	-.22	-.01	-.11	.49*	-.13
Watches tv news rarely	-.05	-.07	.19*	-.14	.07	-.08	.01
Discusses politics rarely	-.10	-.02	.09	.03	-.05	.18	-.10
Politically inactive	.19	-.02	.02	.02	.08	-.01	-.09*
No expertise	—	-.01	-1.25	-.09	.11*	-.00	-.06
Tacit Theories							
President is cause	—	—	—	—	-.08	-.01	.10
President is cure	—	—	—	—	-.11	-.05	-.01
Number of participants	28	43	43	43	62	59	62

*p < .20

**p < .05

indicate whether the priming effect triggered by news coverage is enhanced, diminished, or no different among various types of viewers. A positively signed, statistically significant coefficient indicates that priming is greater for the type of viewer in question. For example, the table entry of +.24 for education in experiment 1 reveals that the priming effect of news coverage was greater for those with a high school education than for those with at least some college experience, but that the difference did not reach statistical significance. (Details on the computation and interpretation of these coefficients are provided in Appendix B.)

Table 10.1 makes clear that priming is not related in any consistent way to education. Sometimes viewers with little formal education were primed a bit more by television news coverage, sometimes they were primed a bit less. This corresponds to what we found for agenda-setting: that against the power of television news, education by itself offers little protection.

We did find sharp and consistent partisan differences, however. For agenda-setting, it may be recalled, the big difference was between partisans and independents: Democrats and Republicans were less susceptible to agenda-setting than were those who identified with neither party. But for priming, the big difference was between Democrats and Republicans.[4] Democrats were primed more effectively by news about the environment, unemployment, and civil rights. Republicans were primed more effectively by news about inflation, unemployment, arms control, and defense. This pattern corresponds rather well to the priorities and policies pursued by the two parties. Over the last several decades protecting the environment, keeping unemployment low, and extending rights and opportunities to black Americans have been largely Democratic priorities, while restraining inflation and maintaining American military strength have been Republican preoccupations. These results suggest that television news primes most effectively those viewers who are predisposed to accept the message in the first place. Democrats are primed more by stories about the environment than are Republicans, perhaps because they need little convincing that the condition of the natural environment represents an important and legitimate problem. Television coverage simply reminds them of what they already know. Similarly, Republicans are primed more by stories about defense than are Democrats, perhaps because the need for a strong defense already figures prominently in their list of priorities. Coverage need not change their minds so much as draw attention to what they know to be true.

The coefficients displayed in table 10.1 also indicate that priming is largely independent of the viewer's involvement in politics. Just seven of the forty-eight separate tests summarized in the table approach significance ($p < .20$, 2-tailed t-test), a record no better than chance. Five of the seven coefficients are positive, indicating that priming is greater among the politically uninvolved. While this tendency is consistent with the results on agenda-setting from chapter 6, it is so slight that we do not take it seriously. The dominant finding is no relationship at all. With respect to political involvement, then, priming appears to be pervasive: it does not diminish among viewers who follow public affairs closely, who scour their newspapers for information about politics, who watch television news religiously, who talk about politics incessantly, who take part in politics energetically, or who know a lot about the problems under consideration. In contrast to agenda-setting, priming flourishes among the politically involved and uninvolved alike.[5]

Finally, and contrary to expectations, we found no support for the idea that priming would be accentuated among those whose tacit theories of national problems implicated the president. Priming was no greater (in experiment 8) among viewers who declared that the president was at least partially to blame for the particular problems emphasized by television newscasts, nor among viewers who said that the president was at least partially responsible for providing remedies for such problems.

This puzzling result prompted a further investigation. Perhaps tacit theories do matter, but only if they are accessible. That is, not only must a viewer possess an appropriate theory—in this case, one that implicates the president—but the viewer must put that theory to use. Surely viewers differ not only in the content of their theories (some implicating the president and some not), but also in the degree to which their theories are accessible (Fiske and Kinder 1981). For some viewers, beliefs that tie a political problem and a president together are casual and poorly formulated. If such beliefs constitute a "theory" at all, it is a theory that is unlikely to be put to much cognitive use. For others, beliefs about national problems and the president reflect the outcome of careful and extensive thought. Such beliefs constitute a theory with real consequences, one that viewers are likely to draw on frequently as they try to manage the daily flow of news.

In order to see whether priming would be strengthened among viewers whose theories both implicated the president and were accessible, we made use of a question asked of participants on the last day of experiment 8. Each participant was invited to recall what they could about the newscasts they had seen over the preceding week.[6] We reasoned that those with accessible theories would be able to remember more from the stories we had implanted in the broadcasts, all of which tied the target problem closely to the policies of the president. Hence our prediction is that priming will be strengthened among viewers who possess a theory that both implicates the president and is accessible, with accessibility measured crudely by the ability to recall bits and pieces from relevant news stories.

The results of this test support the prediction in two of three instances (see Appendix B for details). Specifically, priming was enhanced among viewers who saw the president as at least partly responsible for the arms race and who were able to recall information about the arms race from stories they had seen the previous week. Similarly, priming was enhanced among viewers who saw the president as somehow entangled in problems of civil rights—either as contributing to current problems or as responsible for solving them in the future—and who were able to recall information about civil rights from stories we had inserted into their broadcasts. These results suggest that the theories that viewers hold about national problems do influence their vulnerability to priming. Priming is greatest when viewers are predisposed, by virtue of a well-developed, accessible theory, to see a connection between the president's responsibilities and the condition of the country.

CONCLUSION

Priming, like agenda-setting, depends not only on the message, but also on the audience. The nature of this dependence in the two cases is quite different, however. The audience characteristic that mattered most for agenda-setting was political involvement. Agenda-setting was greatest among those viewers with limited political skills and interests. In contrast, television news primes the politically involved just as effectively as it does the politically withdrawn. Involvement offers resources against agenda-setting, but no protection against priming.

This contrast may reflect the more subtle nature of priming as compared with agenda-setting. While effective agenda-setting merely requires that television news command the viewer's attention, priming requires a second step. Not only must viewers focus on a particular problem, they must also realize that the problem has implications for their evaluation of the president. The politically involved may differ from their uninvolved counterparts in opposite ways during the two steps, so that overall differences between them are canceled. In the first step, the involved may be *less* likely to be captured by the focus of television news (consistent with the results on agenda-setting reported in chapter 6). But in the second step, they may be *more* likely to see the connections between the problem and the president.[7] In short, the involved tend to be less susceptible to priming because they are less likely to be swayed by the day-to-day focus of television news, and more susceptible to priming by virtue of their greater inclination toward performance-based evaluation. Because involvement cuts both ways, the attentive and the disengaged end up equally—and acutely— vulnerable to priming.

Although involvement does not condition susceptibility, partisan attachments and theories of national problems do. Priming is strengthened among Democrats for problems that are prominent on the agenda of the Democratic Party, among Republicans for problems that are prominent on the agenda of the Republican Party, and among viewers who possess well-developed theories that tie national problems and the president together.

The strongest results of all are associated with partisanship. These results are interesting for what they reveal about priming directly, but also for their contrast with how they might reasonably have turned out. For example, one reasonable expectation for partisan differences in priming would maintain that opponents of the incumbent president's party would be primed more effectively, at least by "bad" news, than would supporters of the president's party. Indeed, the opponents should be willing victims of priming: Democrats should be happy to blame an incumbent Republican president for whatever is going wrong, while Republicans would be expected to return the favor when a Democrat holds the office. But this is not what we found. With Reagan as president, Democrats showed the effects of priming less than did Republicans when presented with chilling news of the arms race. Similarly, with Carter as president, Republicans manifested less priming than did Democrats when presented with powerful accounts of the deteriorating environment. In short, the partisan differences in priming we detected were quite subtle and did not correspond to a simple partisan allocation of blame and credit.

A second contrast is with the partisan effects we found in agendasetting in chapter 6. Although partisanship influences both agendasetting and priming, it does so in different ways. For agenda-setting, the sharp contrast was between Independents and partisans: Independents were influenced more and partisans less, presumably because the political priorities of partisans were anchored more securely. For priming, the sharp contrast was between types of partisans—between Democrats and Republicans—presumably because Democrats and Republicans differ in the importance they grant to various national problems. This contrast implies, as do the results reported throughout this chapter, that agenda-setting and priming constitute related but distinct manifestations of the political power of television news.

Such power is not unlimited. The relationships between priming on the one hand and partisan attachments and tacit theories on the other suggest some limits to priming. Both relationships imply that priming is reduced among those who are not predisposed in the direction of the priming story. Democrats confronted with news about "Republican" problems, like Republicans confronted with news about "Democratic" problems, are less readily primed. Similarly, those whose theories about national problems are either poorly formed or do not include links between the problem and the president are as a consequence less vulnerable to priming. Putting these results together with those from preceding chapters, it would appear that priming depends both upon features of the news presentation and features of the audience. Priming is greatest when the news frames a particular problem as if it were the president's business, when viewers are prepared to regard the problem as important, and when they see the problem as entangled in the duties and obligations of the presidency.

Electoral Consequences
of Priming

Candidates for public office go to extraordinary lengths in order to "make news." They schedule their time and arrange their activities to fit the organizational needs and standard routines of the news media. They attempt to enhance the amount of attention they receive and control the terms in which they are covered. In doing so, candidates hope to prime voters' choices to their own advantage. The experiments reported in this chapter provide a partial assessment of how realistic such hopes are. Here we extend our investigation of priming to elections—and therefore to the core of democracy—examining both a congressional and a presidential campaign. In each instance our purpose is to illuminate the relationship between the preoccupations of television news and the decisions voters make on election day.

VOTING IN U.S. HOUSE ELECTIONS

By the standards of presidential elections and certainly by the standards of civics textbooks, the votes citizens cast in House elections appear ill-informed and lightly-considered. Most voters know rather little about their incumbent representative and even less about the candidates who challenge them (Stokes and Miller 1962; Mann and Wolfinger 1980). No doubt this reflects both the peripheral place of congressional elections in people's lives and the light coverage typically allocated to congressional campaigns (Behr 1985; Clarke and Evans 1983). In such circumstances of low interest and limited information, voters appear to follow simple rules of thumb. In particular, they tend to support candidates of their own party (somewhat less now than a quarter-century ago [Stokes and Miller 1962; Mann and Wolfinger 1980]), and they tend to support incumbents of any party (increasingly so [Cover and Mayhew 1977; Jacobson 1981]). Party and incumbency are the dominant considerations in House elections.

However, two other considerations may also come into play—especially, we suspect, if they are primed. One is the voter's assessment of national economic conditions. When the economy sputters,

House candidates of the president's party do poorly; when times are good, such candidates do well (Kramer 1971; Tufte 1978; Kinder and Kiewiet 1979, 1981). The other is the voter's assessment of the personal qualities of the candidates themselves. When asked what they like and dislike about House candidates, voters refer most often to leadership qualities (or more commonly to their absence), to competence and experience, and to various other personal attributes (Jacobson 1981; Mann and Wolfinger 1980).

In short, voting in House elections reflects a mix of partisanship, incumbency, national economic conditions, and the personal qualities of the candidates. We propose that the relative importance of these various considerations depends partly on how intensively each is primed. Voters exposed to local news broadcasts that focus on the national economy should be guided especially by their assessments of national economic conditions. Voters whose local news programs focus on the House candidates should be especially likely to choose according to their appraisals of the personal qualities of the candidates. Voters exposed to local newscasts that emphasize neither should rely especially on party and incumbency.

EXPERIMENT 10 AND THE RACE FOR CONGRESS IN CONNECTICUT'S THIRD DISTRICT

To test for priming effects in congressional elections, we embedded an experiment within the final days of the 1982 midterm House election in the third district of Connecticut.[1] The Third district spreads across south central Connecticut and includes the city of New Haven. The 1982 contest pitted Lawrence DeNardis, the Republican first-term incumbent, against Bruce Morrison, the liberal Democratic challenger. Experiment 10, run in sequence style, began on October 25 and ended on October 30, three days prior to election day. Participants were recruited in the usual fashion with the additional stipulation that they be registered voters (91 percent of those recruited were in fact registered). Participants were randomly assigned to one of three treatment conditions, each offering a slightly different rendition of the evening *local* television news.

In the first, each day participants watched a half-hour newscast that included a 3–5 minute segment devoted to the candidates. These stories dealt with positions on public issues taken by DeNardis and Morrison, the groups that had endorsed them, and their personal backgrounds. In one story, for example, the reporter announced that a local teachers' union had endorsed DeNardis. Viewers were then shown excerpts from a debate in which both candidates talked about the endorsement and their positions on federal aid to education.

Participants in the second condition watched the identical news shows, except that stories about the candidates were replaced by stories about the economy. Most of these segments drew direct connections between the state of the economy, President Reagan's policies, and the midterm elections. For example, one piece featured President Reagan urging voters to "stay the course," while another indicated that the Democrats were anticipating significant victories because of "Reaganomics" and high unemployment.

Participants assigned to the third condition constituted a neutral comparison group. They watched the same local broadcasts, but purged of any references to the candidates, the economy, or the impending election.

Our major interest here, of course, is in priming. We need to determine whether differences in the focus of local television news over the course of a week led to systematic differences in the criteria voters applied in selecting their representative. In the shadowy world of House elections, however, local television news may serve a more elementary function as well. Because voters typically know so little about the candidates who compete to represent them in Washington, a week's worth of campaign coverage may be quite instructive. Voters may become more informed about who the candidates are, which party they represent, the issues that divide them, and so forth. We will therefore assess whether television news coverage not only primes but also informs the voter.

INFORMING CONGRESSIONAL VOTERS

One day after the last newscast, participants were asked to identify the party affiliations of the two candidates. Only 56 percent of the participants assigned to the control condition (who saw no stories about the candidates) knew that DeNardis was the Republican and that Morrison was the Democrat. Meanwhile, virtually *all* participants assigned to the candidate condition—94 percent—correctly associated DeNardis and Morrison with their parties.[2]

Participants were also asked whether there was anything in particular that they liked about each candidate, and, in a separate question, whether there was anything in particular they disliked about each. As expected, people assigned to the candidate condition had more to say in response to these questions than did those assigned to the control condition. This difference between conditions was somewhat greater in the case of viewers' comments about Morrison, the challenger, than about DeNardis, the incumbent.[3]

Participants were then asked the degree to which they agreed with first DeNardis and then Morrison on a series of five policy questions: nuclear arms control, social security, unemployment, defense spending, and federal aid to education. We expected the proportion of viewers who felt unable to say whether they agreed or not to be comparatively large in the control condition, and so it was: 44 percent of those assigned to the neutral condition could not indicate their level of agreement with DeNardis on all five policy questions, as compared to just 26 percent of those assigned to the candidate condition. This difference was somewhat sharper in participants' judgments of policy agreement with Morrison: the corresponding figures there were 44 percent and 16 percent.[4]

Finally, we examined the extent to which our participants had an impression of the candidates' personal qualities. Participants were asked how well each of eleven personality characteristics described DeNardis and then how well each described Morrison. As expected, participants who watched news broadcasts that paid attention to the candidates were more prepared to offer personality judgments than were those who watched news broadcasts that gave no attention to the candidates (although the differences were surprisingly small). Participants assigned to the candidate condition answered on average 65 percent of the trait questions posed to them about DeNardis and 61 percent of the trait questions posed to them about Morrison. Among participants assigned to the control condition, these averages fell off to 60 percent and 53 percent, respectively.[5]

In summary, we find modest but consistent differences in the anticipated direction. Voters assigned to local news that provided significant coverage of the House candidates knew more about them than did their counterparts whose broadcasts ignored the candidates: they were more able to identify (correctly) the candidates' party affiliation; they had more to say about each candidate and seemed to know more (or at least felt they knew more) about the candidates' policy stands and personal characteristics.[6] Although never decisively so, the differences were generally a bit sharper in participants' impressions of Morrison than of DeNardis. Since incumbents are typically much better known than challengers (Mann and Wolfinger 1980), our experimental intervention conveyed, in effect, more information about Morrison than DeNardis.

We also looked for differences in how much participants knew about the state of the national economy, the focus of the other experimental treatment, but in vain. Participants were asked whether the national economy had improved, declined, or stayed about the same over the past year; and whether the economy would likely improve, decline, or stay about the same over the next year. They were also asked to evaluate President Reagan's success in managing economic problems, and then to judge whether economic problems could generally be dealt with more effectively by Democrats or by Republicans. Participants exposed to news coverage of the economy were no more prepared to answer such questions than were participants who saw no economic news during the experiment. Instead, virtually *everyone*, regardless of treatment, expressed an opinion on virtually *every* economic question. Evidently, our experimental manipulation regarding national economic conditions merely duplicated information participants had already gleaned from other sources—from newspapers, magazines, national television news, day-to-day conversations, and their own experiences.[7]

PRIMING CONGRESSIONAL VOTERS

Another and quite separate question is whether the experimentally-induced emphasis upon the state of the economy affected the importance voters attached to the economy in deciding between DeNardis and Morrison. This is the standard priming hypothesis and we examine it next. In fact, we test three separate propositions, each a specific incarnation of priming. First, do viewers exposed to news about the economy rely more heavily on their assessments of economic conditions when reaching their vote decision, in comparison to viewers exposed to news about the candidates or to no news of the election at all? Second, do viewers exposed to coverage of the candidates grant more importance to the qualities they admired in the candidates than do viewers in either of the other two treatments? And third, do viewers given no information about the campaign rely more heavily on partisanship and incumbency than do viewers in the economy and candidate treatments?

To answer these questions we obviously need to know how participants voted. Here we took an indirect route. Each participant was asked to evaluate both DeNardis and Morrison on a one hundred-point "thermometer" scale, on which zero degrees means a very negative evaluation (extremely cold), one hundred degrees means a very positive evaluation (extremely warm), and fifty degrees means a neutral or ambivalent evaluation. Previous election studies have demonstrated a close connection between the thermometer ratings citizens make of the contending candidates shortly before the election and the votes they eventually cast (e.g., Brody and Page 1973; Mann 1978), and so it was in the Third District in 1982. As expected, the net difference in participants' thermometer ratings of DeNardis and Morrison predicted their preferences nearly perfectly: fifty-five of fifty-six participants intended to vote for the candidate they rated more warmly.[8] Because thermometer ratings predict vote so powerfully, and because they provide a more sensitive measure, we will use thermometer ratings in our test of priming as a surrogate for the vote itself.

In keeping with the extensive literature on congressional elections, we presume that voters arrive at their ratings of the two candidates (and therefore their votes) by taking into account four considerations: the candidates' party affiliations,[9] their comparative visibility (a measure of the incumbent's advantage),[10] the candidates' personal qualities,[11] and national economic conditions.[12] As a rule, Republicans will prefer DeNardis while Democrats will prefer Morrison; voters who recognize DeNardis, but not Morrison, will give their support to the former; voters will support the candidate in whom they see the greater number of admirable qualities; and, finally, voters who take a grim view of the economy will prefer Morrison, while those more optimistic about economic conditions will prefer DeNardis. These relationships should hold for voters in general, regardless of which rendition of the local news they watched. But if the priming hypothesis holds, then the impact of economic conditions should increase when local news focuses on the nation's economy, the impact of the personal qualities of candidates should increase when local news focuses on the candidates, and the impact of party and incumbency should increase, by default, when local news focuses on neither the economy nor the candidates.

Our analysis sustains the first two predictions but not the third (see Appendix B for estimation details). As the results in table 11.1 indicate, judgments of national economic conditions predicted thermometer ratings powerfully, regardless of experimental condition. Even when not primed by economic news, voters who were more optimistic

TABLE 11.1

Priming Congressional Voting: The Estimated Impact of Economic Conditions and Candidate Qualities on Evaluation of Congressional Candidates as a Function of TV News Coverage: Experiment 10 (ordinary least squares estimates)

	No TV Coverage (Baseline)	TV Coverage (Primed)	Difference: Primed Minus Baseline
Economic assessments	3.08	10.49	7.41*
Candidate qualities	6.45	31.07	24.62*

*$p < .01$

about national economic conditions preferred DeNardis over Morrison more often than did those who were more pessimistic about the economy. In more concrete terms, a difference of four points on the index of economic optimism (the difference between mild optimism and mild pessimism) was associated with a thermometer rating difference of about twelve degrees in DeNardis's favor. This is a noteworthy difference, but—and this is the important point—one that grows substantially larger among voters exposed to news about the economy. When viewers were primed with economic news, the impact of economic assessments on evaluations of the candidates more than tripled: a difference of four points on the index of economic optimism translated into a DeNardis advantage of over forty degrees.

An even stronger priming effect emerged with respect to candidate qualities. Unremarkably, viewers who saw more positive qualities in DeNardis than Morrison felt more warmly toward DeNardis, even when their local broadcasts ignored the candidates entirely. Such viewers who mentioned two positive qualities about DeNardis but who could think of nothing they liked about Morrison rated the former more warmly, on average, by some thirteen degrees. But among viewers primed with information about the candidates, the impact of this same difference increased nearly fivefold. Now viewers with nothing good to say about Morrison who cited two favorable qualities about DeNardis rated the latter more warmly on the thermometer by more than sixty degrees. This is a huge and politically consequential priming effect.

Contrary to expectations, we found no support for the prediction that incumbency and party would both grow more powerful when voters were not "distracted" by news about the economy or information about the candidates. Voters who could name DeNardis but not Morrison gave the incumbent a ten-point advantage in the thermometer ratings, compared to viewers who were able to name both, but this advantage was not accentuated among viewers exposed to no information about the campaign. And we could find no effect of party identification in any condition. Once we took into account the effects of voters' assessments of national economic conditions and their appraisal of and familiarity with the two candidates, the direct impact of party identification disappeared entirely.

Party identification did have strong *indirect* effects, however, shaping both voters' assessments of national economic conditions and their impressions of the candidates. Democrats expressed more pessimistic opinions about the nation's economy than did Republicans; similarly, they said more nice things about Morrison than DeNardis. Thus, party identification did contribute to voters' thermometer ratings of the candidates, but indirectly. Furthermore, these indirect effects of party identification were strengthened by the focus of news coverage, just as the priming hypothesis would suggest. On the one hand, the impact of party identification on views of national economic conditions increased among viewers assigned to local news devoted to the national economy. That is, compared to Republicans, Democrats were more pessimistic in their economic assessments and more critical of the Reagan administration's economic performance when local news focused on national economic conditions.[13] On the other hand, the impact of party identification on appraisals of the two candidates increased among viewers assigned to local news devoted to the candidates. That is, compared to Republicans, Democrats had more nice things to say about Morrison than about DeNardis when the local news focused on the candidates.[14]

The electoral consequence of the kinds of priming effects we have detected here can be very substantial. Depending upon the mixture of other forces at work in a campaign, they may even be decisive. For illustrative purposes, consider voters in Connecticut's Third District who recognized both DeNardis and Morrison and were ambivalent toward them (i.e., they named as many positive qualities for DeNardis as for Morrison). Such voters who were also modestly upbeat about the national economy, according to our analysis, would tend to support DeNardis. But DeNardis could count on their support to a much greater degree if the voters received news about the nation's economy than if they watched news that emphasized the candidates. We estimate that a hypothetical voter would have preferred DeNardis by forty-six degrees in the first instance and by just ten degrees in the second. The contrast is almost as striking in the case of the hypothetical voter who is pessimistic about the national economy. Our experimental results predict that if exposed to news about the candidates, this voter would have preferred Morrison by a slight margin (nine degrees on the average), but if exposed to coverage of the economy, would have preferred Morrison by a rather comfortable margin (seventeen degrees on the average).

These projections from our experimental results suggest that voters can be moved from indecision to strong preference depending only on the coverage that television news provides. It is not unreasonable to conclude that priming may sometimes determine who wins and who loses. In the Third District in 1982, Lawrence DeNardis spent over $300,000 and received more than eighty-eight thousand votes. It was not quite enough. With 50.5 percent of the vote, Morrison was elected; DeNardis was sent home.[15]

VOTING IN PRESIDENTIAL ELECTIONS

We turn next to the part priming might play in presidential elections. From the voters' perspective, contests for the presidency are nothing if not complex. They are partly a clash between the major parties, partly an ideological struggle over the policies government should pursue, partly a judgment on the administration's performance over the past four years and a comparative appraisal of what sorts of people the candidates seem to be, partly a reflection of the particular feelings that the candidates evoke, and much more. Because so many elements may plausibly enter into the voter's choice, the prospects for priming seem great.

THE CASE OF 1980

The 1980 presidential campaign may be a particularly telling case in point. Recall that as election day neared, the race for the presidency seemed too close to call. By most accounts Ronald Reagan was ahead, but his lead over President Carter was tiny, and the unusually large number of undecided voters made the contest difficult to predict. In election-eve surveys with large samples of probable voters, the CBS-*New York Times* poll found Reagan ahead by a single percentage point; the ABC-Harris poll reported Reagan's lead to be five percentage points; the Gallup Poll had Reagan ahead by three points. A few days later, Reagan won decisively, receiving 51 percent of the vote to Carter's 41 percent. Why did the polls perform so poorly?

One possibility is that the polls were basically correct, but that large numbers of voters shifted toward Reagan between the time the interviewing was completed and election day. Most conspicuous in the campaign's final days was the chain of events that appeared to promise the resolution of the Iranian hostage crisis. These developments, and the ultimate collapse of the negotiations, were given enormous and detailed attention by the press. On the night before the election, the three network news programs each devoted much of their broadcasts to a recapitulation of the Iranian crisis, the taking of the American embassy in Teheran, the months of stalled negotiations, the failure of the rescue mission, and especially the multiplying complexities involved in meeting the Iranians' demands. Perhaps such coverage dealt a devastating and fatal blow to the President's reelection chances, inducing many voters to conceive of the decision they confronted as a referendum on the Carter presidency's performance on foreign affairs.[16]

This claim is certainly congenial to our theoretical perspective. It is simply a particular—though particularly consequential—version of priming. And the results of the experiments reported so far are consistent with it. We can go further, however. Our final experiment was designed to reconstruct the priming effects, if any, associated with the intensive coverage of the Iranian crisis in the closing days of the 1980 presidential contest.

AN EXPERIMENTAL RECONSTRUCTION OF THE 1980 CAMPAIGN

Experiment 7 was conducted in June of 1982. Participants were recruited from the New Haven community in the usual fashion and randomly assigned to one of three treatment conditions. Participants in the neutral or control treatment were shown a collection of nine recent network news stories compiled from the Vanderbilt University Television News Archive. Participants assigned to the hostage treatment saw the identical set, with two exceptions. Instead of a story on the endangered status of the California Condor, they watched a story from the final days of the 1980 campaign that described Iranian demands for the release of the hostages, concluding with Iran's threat that if such demands were not met, the hostages would be tried as spies. Then in place of a story devoted to the trans-Siberian railroad, hostage treatment participants watched a clip that featured Ayatollah Khomeini addressing militant students in Teheran while the correspondent described Iran as waiting to hear from Washington regarding its demands.

The major purpose of experiment 7 was to assess whether viewers primed with hostage crisis news stories relied upon foreign affairs in evaluating President Carter's overall performance more heavily than did those in the neutral treatment. An additional purpose was to see whether priming can be produced by good news as well as by bad. Participants randomly assigned to a third treatment saw the same broadcasts, but this time with two stories inserted that recapitulated Jimmy Carter's greatest triumph in foreign affairs—the signing of the Camp David Peace Accords. This treatment will enable us to ascertain whether stories that focus on achievements can trigger priming, just as stories that focus on failures can.

We tested for priming in experiment 7 by comparing the impact of viewers' ratings of Carter's performance in foreign affairs on their assessment of his overall performance as president across the three experimental conditions. We actually examined priming in four separate tests, each involving a distinct component of Carter's foreign affairs performance. Participants were asked to evaluate: (1) President Carter's management of the hostage crisis (most thought he had bungled it); (2) his performance at the Camp David Middle East negotiations (most gave him high marks); (3) the power and moral authority exercised around the world by the United States under the Carter administration (most viewers thought that U.S. influence had declined); and, finally, (4) President Carter's effectiveness in dealing with world problems (most believed Carter only modestly effective).[17] If the priming hypothesis is correct, each of these aspects of Carter's foreign affairs performance should exert a greater impact on general assessments of the Carter presidency when television news dwells upon foreign affairs.

The results from the first two tests, those that involve specific aspects of President Carter's performance in foreign affairs, are displayed in table 11.2. (See Appendix B for details on estimation.) They demonstrate that priming can indeed be triggered by achievements as well as by problems. Stories about Carter's success at Camp David raised the significance of foreign affairs performance just as did stories that recapitulated the sorry history of the hostage crisis.

The results also suggest that priming requires a close correspondence between the judgment to be primed and the news story that triggers the priming. The importance accorded to Carter's management of the hostage crisis in evaluations of his overall performance was magnified by exposure to news about the crisis, but not by exposure to news about Camp David. In complementary fashion, the impact of viewers' evaluations of Carter's management of the Camp David treaty on their evaluations of his overall performance was materially enhanced by exposure to Camp David broadcasts, less by hostage crisis stories.

Table 11.3 moves the tests of priming to a more general plane. One recurring theme in the 1980 presidential campaign was the alleged decline of American influence in world affairs, a theme that the Reagan campaign stressed repeatedly and which the hostage crisis seemed to

TABLE 11.2

Priming Presidential Evaluations: The Impact of Hostage Crisis and Camp David Performance on Evaluations of President Carter's Overall Performance as a Function of TV News Coverage: Experiment 7 (ordinary least squares estimates)

	TV Coverage of Camp David	No TV Coverage (Baseline)	TV Coverage of Hostage Crisis
Camp David performance	.43*	.08	.30
Hostage crisis performance	.37	.31	.53*

*$p < .20$ (for difference between primed and baseline impact)

typify. Row 1 indicates whether news about the hostage crisis (or about Camp David) strengthened the extent to which viewers measured the Carter presidency against this standard. The answer is a resounding *no:* row 1 reveals not a trace of priming. Notice that the theme of declining American influence in world affairs *was* important. Viewers who believed that the position of the U.S. overseas had eroded during Carter's tenure evaluated Mr. Carter much less favorably on average than did viewers who believed the United States was as respected abroad during the Carter Administration as ever. But this substantial relationship was not augmented by television coverage of foreign affairs.

The results presented across the second row of table 11.3 suggest that this failure is due not to the sheer generality of the theme of declining American influence overseas, but to its content. Row 2 indicates considerable priming at work on judgments of President Carter's effectiveness in dealing with foreign countries, the second general theme. And once again, priming is induced both by presidential achievements as well as by presidential problems. In each instance, moreover, the effect is substantial. Exposure to news about Camp David or about the hostage crisis produced a *doubling* of the impact of ratings of Carter's effectiveness in dealing with foreign nations on evaluations of his overall performance as president.

A sense of how sizable these priming effects are can be had from the following exercise. Suppose two prospective voters, Smith and Jones, are identical in all ways except that Smith judges President Carter to have been generally effective in dealing with foreign countries (a score of two on our five-point scale) while Jones judges the President to have been generally ineffective (a score of four). If Smith and Jones were assigned together to the control condition in our experiment, this one

TABLE 11.3

Priming Presidential Evaluations: The Impact of Sense of U.S. Decline and Carter's Effectiveness with Foreign Countries on Evaluations of President Carter's Overall Performance as a Function of TV News Coverage: Experiment 7 (ordinary least squares estimates)

	TV Coverage of Camp David	No TV Coverage (Baseline)	TV Coverage of Hostage Crisis
U.S. decline	.63	.65	.60
Carter's effectiveness with foreign countries	.57*	.30	.69**

$*p < .20$ (for difference between primed and baseline impact)

$**p < .05$

difference would translate into a modest difference in their overall evaluation of President Carter's performance: Smith would have a slightly positive overall evaluation of Mr. Carter while Jones would be slightly negative. If, instead, Smith and Jones viewed television news stories about the hostage crisis, the difference of one point in their ratings of Carter's effectiveness in foreign relations would be much more consequential. Having been primed with stories about the Iranian crisis, Smith would now evaluate President Carter rather positively while Jones's evaluation would be sharply negative. Such a difference begins to suggest the part priming might play in presidential election outcomes in general and in the 1980 presidential contest in particular.[18]

SUMMARY AND CONCLUSION

Our pair of election experiments shows that priming operates on the choices voters make. The priorities that are uppermost in voters' minds as they go to the polls to select a president or a U.S. Representative appear to be powerfully shaped by the last-minute preoccupations of television news.

One reason for the strength of these effects may be that our news manipulations focused on events, outcomes, or considerations for which the candidates were unquestionably responsible. As we found in chapter 9, priming is enhanced when news coverage interprets events in such a way as to imply an intimate connection between the events and the target of judgment. Our two election experiments fulfill this condition amply. The study of the 1982 midterm House election focused either on the personal qualities of the candidates—for which the candidates are obviously responsible—or on national economic conditions, aggressively framed so as to invite viewers to draw a connection between national economic policy and the composition of the Congress. And our experimental analogue of the final days of the 1980 presidential campaign emphasized either the Camp David Accords or the hostage crisis, both of which were widely interpreted as President Carter's personal triumph and tragedy, respectively. From this point of view, the magnitude of the results may seem understandable, if no less unsettling.

The election-day experiment contained two further lessons that bear repeating here. In the first place, priming can apparently be set off by achievements as well as by failures. Flattering stories about the Camp David Accords were just as effective in triggering priming in viewers' evaluations of President Carter as were grim stories about the hostage crisis. We do not mean to suggest, based on a single comparison, that achievements and failures will always be equally and symmetrically effective. Rather we regard this one result merely as a demonstration that priming can be triggered by both bad news and good news.

A second lesson is that priming may require a close fit between the domain of judgment that is the intended target of priming and the news stories that constitute the prime itself. This is suggested by two results. First, the importance granted President Carter's handling of the hostage crisis in the President's overall evaluation was enhanced by exposure to hostage crisis stories, but not by exposure to Camp David stories. Similarly, the impact of viewers' evaluations of Carter's success at Camp David on their evaluations of his overall performance was enhanced substantially by exposure to Camp David broadcasts, less by hostage crisis stories. Second, coverage of either the Camp David Peace Accords or the negotiations regarding the release of the hostages that took place during the 1980 campaign's last days induced viewers to weigh President Carter's effectiveness in dealing with foreign countries more heavily in their overall judgment of his performance as president, but *not* to weigh any more heavily the theme of American decline in world affairs. The first—Carter's international effectiveness—is directly and strongly implicated by the triumph of Camp David and the collapse of the Iranian negotiations. The second—the United States's declining power and prestige—is also implied, but less directly and less strongly. In the latter instance, more inferential work is required on the viewer's part, work that evidently few viewers were prepared to undertake. These results suggest that in some respects the public is admirably discriminating. Priming appears to depend heavily on how closely the pictures and stories that appear in the news correspond to the choices and judgments viewers are called upon to make.

By the verdict of this chapter, television news exerts a powerful influence on the electoral process. Should this influence be welcomed or deplored? Does television news contribute to democracy or undermine it? Without promising definitive answers, we take up such question in the next and final chapter. Our purpose there is to draw out the implications of our findings for the practice and promise of democratic politics in the age of television.

News That Matters

Not so very long ago, television was "nothing but a gleam in the entre-preneurial eye" (Weaver 1975, 81). No longer. In just four decades, it has become a comfortable and easy habit, a settled and central institution. As television has moved to the center of American life, TV news has become Americans' single most important source of information about political affairs. The purpose of our effort has been to provide a systematic examination of this new relationship. In this final chapter we summarize our principal results and position them within the context of the broader literature on mass communication and politics. We argue that, for good or ill, television news has become a regular partici-pant in the American political process. Finally, as a means of assessing the normative implications of our results for a democratic society, we discuss the ways in which television news conveys unusual and distinc-tive views of politics—views that eventually become our own.

Recapitulation of Results

Agenda-Setting

Americans' views of their society and nation are powerfully shaped by the stories that appear on the evening news. We found that people who were shown network broadcasts edited to draw attention to a particu-lar problem assigned greater importance to that problem—greater im-portance than they themselves did before the experiment began, and greater importance than did people assigned to control conditions that emphasized different problems. Our subjects regarded the target problem as more important for the country, cared more about it, be-lieved that government should do more about it, reported stronger feelings about it, and were much more likely to identify it as one of the country's most important problems. Such differences were apparent immediately after conclusion of the broadcasts one day later, and one week later. They emerged in experiments explicitly designed to test agenda-setting and in experiments designed with other purposes in mind; in sequential experiments that drew the viewer's attention to the

112

problem each day for a week and in assemblage experiments that lasted but one hour; and for a broad array of problems: defense, pollution, arms control, civil rights, energy, social security, drugs, and education. Moreover, these experimental results were generally corroborated by our analysis of trends in network news coverage and national public opinion. That we found essentially the same result using different methods strengthens our conclusion that television news shapes the relative importance Americans attach to various national problems.

To our surprise, the basic agenda-setting effect was not generally enhanced by vivid presentations. If anything, dramatic accounts of personal travails chosen to illustrate national problems appear to undermine agenda-setting, particularly when viewers blame the victims for the troubles that have befallen them. We assume that vivid presentations may enhance agenda-setting, provided viewers regard the victims as innocent. For example, intimate, poignant film of Ethiopian children dying of starvation may drive home the meaning of famine in a way that written accounts cannot. Because such children may be widely understood to be blameless victims of a cruel fate, vivid presentations may add to the viewer's conviction that the African famine is a serious problem. Our results, however, showed only that stories of personal suffering, powerfully depicted, generally did not raise the priority viewers assigned to the target problems.

Our experiments showed that the position of a story in a broadcast did affect agenda-setting. Lead stories were generally more influential than nonlead stories. Our analysis of survey data showed that lead stories exerted a much more profound agenda-setting effect than nonlead stories. We suspect that viewers may simply pay more attention to the first story than to stories that appear later on and that disruptions in viewing are especially likely to occur at home. An alternative explanation of the lead story advantage is that the public may perceive lead stories as being particularly newsworthy. Certainly the networks claim to select the lead story on these grounds.

Television news is, of course, not the only source of information people draw on when thinking about the nation's problems. Another is personal experience. Using both experimental and national survey data, we found that people who encountered problems in their everyday lives were more inclined to see these problems as important for the country as a whole than were individuals not so affected. In particular, we found that blacks attached more importance to civil rights than did whites and that the elderly attached more importance to the viability of the social security system than did the young. When people think of themselves as members of a victimized group, they appear to see their own problems as serious and legitimate ones for the country.

Our special interest in personal predicaments was in the possibility that they might serve as predisposing factors making viewers more vulnerable to a particular news agenda. For the most part, that is just what we found. News coverage of civil rights was more influential among blacks than among whites; coverage of unemployment proved more influential among the unemployed than among the employed;[1] and coverage of the possible bankruptcy of the social security system was a more compelling message for the elderly than for the young. The general point here is that television news appears to be most powerful when it corroborates personal experience, conferring social reinforcement and political legitimacy on the problems and struggles of ordinary life.

Overall, we see our results on agenda-setting as a vindication of Lippmann's observations of more than a half-century ago. Although Lippmann was writing with newspapers in mind, his analysis is nevertheless highly relevant to the place of television news in contemporary American society. His observation that citizens must depend on others for their news about national and world affairs—a world they cannot touch themselves—is amply confirmed here.[2] What we have done is to begin to uncover the various and specific ways that television news determines the citizen's conception of the "mystery off there."

PRIMING

While our agenda-setting results contribute to a long-standing tradition inaugurated by Lippmann and sustained by others, our results in the matter of priming offer a more original perspective. Priming presumes that when evaluating complex political phenomena, people do not take into account all that they know—they cannot, even if they are motivated to do so. Instead, they consider what comes to mind, those bits and pieces of political memory that are accessible. Television news, we supposed, might be a powerful determinant of what springs to mind and what is forgotten or ignored. Through priming (drawing attention to some aspects of political life at the expense of others) television news might help to set the terms by which political judgments are reached and political choices made.

Our results support this claim handsomely. When primed by television news stories that focus on national defense, people judge the president largely by how well he has provided, as they see it, for the nation's defense; when primed by stories about inflation, people evaluate the president by how he has managed, in their view, to keep prices down; and so on. According to a variety of tests, priming is both powerful and pervasive: it emerges in a number of independent tests for arms control, civil rights, defense, inflation, unemployment, and energy; for a Democratic president (Carter) as well as for a Republican one (Reagan); in different experimental arrangements; in response to good news as well as to bad; and in analyses that estimate priming while controlling for the possibility of projection. All this suggests that television news does indeed shape the standards by which presidential performance is measured.

Because our experiments manipulated the attention paid to major national problems, we expected that viewers' judgments of overall presidential performance would be primed more effectively than would assessments of presidential character, whose determinants we assumed were more diverse, an intermixing of the political and the personal. This expectation was confirmed. We also expected that priming would be more pronounced in viewers' assessments of the president's competence than in assessments of his integrity, on the grounds that success or failure in such areas as national defense, inflation, arms control, and the like would reflect more on the president's competence than on his integrity. This expectation was supported in every detail in the case of President Carter but sharply and consistently violated in the case of President Reagan. This unanticipated result suggests that the public may be most susceptible to priming on those aspects of the president's character that are most open to debate. For President Carter, it was a question of competence—was he up to the demands of the job? For President Reagan, it was more a question of trust—did he care for the welfare of all Americans? At a more general level, the aspects of presidential character that the public takes seriously may be determined by the broader political context. Flagrant scandal may underscore trust and integrity, while runaway inflation may feed anxieties about competence and leadership. Should this be so, it would be a case of priming on a historical scale, with potentially historical consequences.

We further found that the power of television news to shape the standards by which presidents are judged is greater when stories focus on the president, and less when stories focus attention elsewhere. When coverage implied that the president was responsible for causing a problem or for solving it, the priming effect increased. When coverage implied that forces and agents other than the president were responsible for the problem, the priming effect diminished. These effects were particularly apparent for problems relatively new to the

American political agenda, for which public understanding is perhaps less solidly formed and therefore more susceptible to the way that television news frames the matter of responsibility.

Our final pair of experiments demonstrate that the networks' agenda also primes the choices voters make. First, voters who were shown local news coverage that emphasized the state of the economy, the president's economic policies, and the implications of such policies for the impending midterm elections, relied heavily on their assessments of economic conditions when deciding which congressional candidate to support. In contrast, voters who watched local broadcasts devoted to the congressional candidates themselves—their positions on policy questions, group endorsements, or personal backgrounds—assigned great importance to these qualities in their choices. These results show that television news (*local* television news in this case) can alter the grounds on which elections are contested. Depending on the interests and resources of local television stations, congressional elections can either be a referendum on the president's economic performance, or purely a local contest between two distinct candidates.[3]

The second experiment moved to the presidential level by reconstructing the intensive coverage lavished upon the Iranian hostage crisis in the closing days of the 1980 presidential campaign. The results suggested, in line with the priming hypothesis, that such coverage encouraged viewers to cast their votes on the basis of President Carter's performance on foreign affairs. Because Carter was widely perceived as ineffectual in his dealings with foreign countries, priming in this case may have dealt a final and fatal blow to the President's reelection chances, transforming an election that appeared breathtakingly close on Saturday into a decisive Republican victory on Tuesday.

MINIMAL EFFECTS REVISITED

Our results imply that television news has become an imposing authority, one that shapes the American public's political conceptions in pervasive ways. This conclusion seems to contradict the minimal effects verdict reached by most empirical research on the political consequences of mass media. How can this discrepancy be understood?

Serious and systematic empirical research on mass media and American politics began in the 1930s, motivated both by the spread of fascism abroad and by what many took to be the sinister proliferation of radio at home. But in a brilliant study of the 1940 presidential election described in *The People's Choice,* Lazarsfeld, Berelson, and Gaudet (1948) concluded that media simply strengthen the predispositions that were already in place prior to the campaign. Meanwhile, an extensive and well-controlled series of experimental studies undertaken during World War II found that films designed to indoctrinate new draftees failed rather spectacularly (Hovland, Lumsdaine, and Sheffield 1949). The avalanche of research on political persuasion that soon followed these path-breaking and ambitious efforts drove home the same point again and again: while propaganda reinforces the public's preferences it does not, and perhaps cannot, change them.[4]

Political persuasion is difficult to achieve, but agenda-setting and priming are apparently pervasive. According to our results, television news clearly and decisively influences the priorities that people attach to various national problems, and the considerations they take into account as they evaluate political leaders or choose between candidates for public office. Had we been interested in studying persuasion, we would have designed other experiments and would have written another book. More likely, we would have written no book at all, since we probably would have had little new to say. That is, had our television news experiments set out to convert Democrats to Republicans, or pro-choice advocates to pro-life advocates, we strongly suspect that the results would have demonstrated yet more evidence in support of minimal effects. Our results on priming in the final days of the 1980 presidential election suggest that persuasion *is* possible, but only under very special circumstances: (1) large numbers of voters remain uncommitted in the closing days of the campaign; (2) late-breaking political events attract considerable media coverage and focus attention on a single aspect of the national condition; and (3) the political developments decisively favor one candidate over the other. But as a general matter, the power of television news—and mass communication in general—appears to rest not on persuasion but on commanding the public's attention (agenda-setting) and defining criteria underlying the public's judgments (priming).

We do not mean to suggest that television's power to set the public agenda and to prime citizens' political choices is unlimited. In fact, our studies suggest clear limits to television's power, which must be kept in mind as we try to decipher the broader significance of our findings.

One limitation is that the agenda-setting effects detected in our experiments were generally confined to the particular problem featured in the edited newscasts. Stories about energy affected beliefs about the importance of energy and energy alone, stories about defense affected beliefs about defense alone, and so on. Such specificity may reflect both the way that the networks typically package the news—in tight, self-contained bundles (Weaver 1972)—and the way that most Americans think about politics, innocent of broad ideological frameworks that might link one national problem with another (Converse 1964; Kinder 1983). Whatever its cause, the specificity of agenda-setting serves to constrain and channel television's influence. Because of the specific nature of the agenda-setting effect, Americans are unlikely to be swept away by any coherent vision of the country's problems. More likely, they will be pushed and pulled in various directions as discrete problems emerge, rise to prominence, and eventually fade away.

Second, Americans are not without informational resources of their own. We found that agenda-setting is weakened among those viewers who are most deeply engaged in public life, presumably because their priorities are more firmly anchored. Because their opinions about the national condition are stronger, they are buffeted less by day-to-day fluctuations in the networks' agendas. We also found that priming is weakened among those who, in effect, are not ready to be primed, by virtue of their partisanship or their tacit theories about national problems. Democrats confronted with news about "Republican" problems, like Republicans confronted with "Democratic" problems, or like viewers whose understanding of national problems is either poorly worked out or does not include links between the president and the problem are, as a consequence, less vulnerable to priming. Television news defines political reality more completely for some Americans than for others.

There is a final and perhaps most important point to make regarding limitations on the power of television news. Each of our experiments on agenda-setting manipulated attention paid to problems that could all plausibly be regarded as relevant to the national interest, each widely understood as having the potential to affect millions of Americans seriously and adversely. Our hunch—unfortunately not tested—is that our experiments could not create concern over *implausible* problems. Had we inserted news stories portraying the discrimination faced by left-handers we very much doubt that viewers would suddenly put aside their worries about unemployment, defense, and environmental degradation. Nor do we think that television news could long sustain a story that was radically at odds with other credible sources of information. In the midst of booming prosperity, could the networks convince Americans that the economy was actually in a shambles? Or, turning the question around, in the depths of a severe recession, could the networks convince the public that times were good? We don't think so, though again we have little direct evidence. We believe that the networks can neither create national problems where there are none nor conceal problems that actually exist. What television news does, instead, is alter the priorities Americans attach to a circumscribed set of problems, all of which are plausible contenders for public concern.

In a parallel way, our experiments on priming reveal that the news reorders the importance viewers attach to various *plausible* standards of political evaluation: our experiments were not designed to test whether network news could induce viewers to apply trivial or irrelevant standards of evaluation to presidents or political candidates. We can only guess that had such experiments been conducted, they would demonstrate that television news cannot induce voters to abandon the traditional standards of evaluation.

In summary, television news shapes the priorities Americans attach to various national problems and the standards they apply to the performance of their government and the qualifications of their leaders. Although subject to limitations (television news cannot create priorities or standards out of thin air) television's power to shape political priorities is nonetheless formidable, as we will see shortly. This view clashes with the romantic ideal of the democratic citizen: one who is informed, skeptical, deeply engaged in public affairs, and thoughtful about the state of the nation and the quality of its leadership. But we know from other evidence that this vision is hopelessly idealistic; in fact, Americans pay casual and intermittent attention to public affairs and are often astonishingly ignorant of the details of contemporary politics (Kinder and Sears 1985).

No doubt a portion of this indifference and ignorance can be attributed to candidates and government officials who practice evasion and deceit, and to the mass media (and especially television news), which operate all too often as if the average American were seven years old. But some of the indifference must be traced to the minor place accorded politics in everyday life. It seems to us highly unreasonable to demand of average citizens that they carefully and skeptically examine news presentations. If politics is ordinarily subordinate to the demands and activities of earning a living, raising a family, and forming and maintaining friendships, then citizens should hardly be expected to spend much of their time and energy each day grappling with the flow of news. How then do Americans "understand" politics?

The answer is that we muddle through. Faced with the enormous complexity and uncertainty of the political world, possessed of neither the motivation nor the wits to optimize, we strike various compromises. We resort to cognitive shortcuts (Tversky and Kahneman 1974) and settle for acceptable solutions (Simon 1955). As a consequence of such compromises, our judgments are often creatures of circumstance. What we think about the federal deficit, turmoil in Latin America, or the performance of our president depends less on what we know in some complete sense and more on what happens to come to mind.

The general moral here is that judgment and choice are inevitably shaped by considerations that are, however briefly, accessible. And when it comes to political judgment and choice, no institution yet devised can compete with television news in determining which considerations come to light and which remain in darkness.

POLITICAL RAMIFICATIONS

Although it was not our purpose to investigate the political ramifications of agenda-setting and priming directly, we nevertheless feel obliged to spell out what we take them to be. In doing so, we are in effect making explicit the assumptions that motivated our research. We undertook the various investigations reported here under the assumption that *if* television news could be shown to be a major force in shaping the viewing public's conception of national life, the political ramifications would be portentous. With the results now in, we believe that through agenda-setting and priming, television news affects the American political process in at last three important ways: first, by determining which problems the government must take up and which it can safely ignore; second, by facilitating or undermining an incumbent president's capacity to govern, and third, by intruding, sometimes dramatically and decisively, upon campaigns and elections.

THE GOVERNMENT'S AGENDA

If television news influences the priorities Americans attach to national problems, and if such priorities eventually shape governmental decision-making, our results on agenda-setting become important for what they reveal about the formation of public policy. The essential question, then, is whether policy makers heed instruction from the general public in selecting which problems to consider and which to ignore.

We believe that public opinion does influence the governmental political agenda. We also agree with V. O. Key, however, that although public opinion influences the focus and direction of government policy, such influence is sharply limited:

The articulation between government and opinion is relatively loose. Parallelism between action and opinion tends not to be precise in matters of detail; it prevails rather with respect to broad purpose. And in the correlation of purpose and action time lags may occur between the crystallization of a sense of mass purpose and its fulfillment in public action. Yet in the long run, majority purpose and public action tend to be brought into harmony (1961, 553).

The "harmonizing" of government policy and public opinion is loose, and sometimes occurs very gradually, partly because ordinary Americans are indifferent to and uninformed about the details of policy, and partly because of the successful intervention of organized interests whose preferences depart from those of the unorganized public (Edelman 1964; McConnell 1966; Schattschneider 1960). Nevertheless, the national government does appear to respond, if slowly and imperfectly, to the public's wishes (e.g., Burstein 1979; Burstein and Freudenburg 1978; Page and Shapiro 1983; Verba and Nie 1972; Weissberg 1976). Thus, television news must assume a significant role in the intricate process by which citizens' inchoate goals and concerns eventually become government policy.

PRESIDENTIAL POWER

Television news may also influence an incumbent president's capacity to govern. As Neustadt (1960) proposed and others have shown (Kernell 1986; Rivers and Rose 1985), presidential power derives partly from public approval. A president who is admired by the people tends to be powerful in Washington. The proliferation of opinion polls has accentuated this connection. Of course, public approval is not the only factor affecting a president's success. But other things being equal, the Congress, the governmental bureaucracy, world leaders, the private sector, and the executive branch itself all become more accommodating to a president who is riding high with the public. As television news shapes the criteria by which the president's performance is measured, so may it indirectly contribute to a president's power.

This point has not escaped presidents and their advisers. Without exception, presidents in the television age have assiduously sought to control the criteria by which they are viewed and evaluated. From the careful staging of news conferences to the manufacturing of pseudo-events, "making news" and "going public" have become essential presidential activities (Kernell 1986). Our findings suggest that presidents would be foolish to do otherwise. To the extent that the president succeeds in focusing public attention on his accomplishments while distracting the public from his mistakes, he contributes to his popularity and, eventually, to the influence he can exercise over national policy.

THE ELECTORAL PROCESS

Finally, our results suggest that by priming some considerations and ignoring others, television news can shift the grounds on which campaigns are contested. Priming may therefore determine who takes office—and with what mandate—and who is sent home. Moreover, election results do matter in tangible ways: elected officials pursue policies that are broadly consistent with the interests of their core political constituencies (e.g., Bunce 1981; Cameron 1977; Hibbs 1977). Consequently, insofar as television news contributes, if unwittingly, to the success of one candidate over another, the results on priming we have uncovered here are politically important.

It seems clear to us that television news has become a major force in the American political process. The problems that government chooses to tackle, the president's power over the focus and direction of national policy, and the real and tangible consequences of elections are all affected by the glare of the television camera. Less clear is whether this influence is necessarily undesirable. Whether, as many maintain, television threatens public opinion and menaces democratic government would seem to turn on the question of how faithfully the pictures and stories that appear on the news each night portray what of real consequence is actually happening in the world, a thorny question that is our next and final topic.

GOOD NEWS OR BAD?

According to the Federal Communications Commission, the basic purpose of American broadcasting is "the development of an informed public opinion through the dissemination of news and ideas concerning the vital public issues of the day" (FCC 1949). How well does television news live up to this mandate? How faithfully and wisely do the networks interpret the "vital public issues of the day"? How close is the correspondence between reality and what many of us, without really thinking about it, take to *be* reality?

To serve the public interest, television news must first choose judiciously when it selects newsworthy events. Unfortunately, the evidence on television's performance in this respect is for the most part fragmentary and anecdotal. One exception is provided by Behr and Iyengar (1985), who found that network coverage of unemployment followed quite closely the current rate of unemployment, that coverage of energy responded strongly to increases in energy costs, and that coverage of inflation responded to surges in prices. These results indicate that television news coverage can sometimes reflect rather well what is actually happening in the country.

It is not clear, however, whether these results and their comforting implications for an informed public opinion can be generalized safely to other problems. The fit between reality and news coverage of energy, unemployment, and inflation could be assessed because objective and more or less respectable indicators of the pertinent real-world conditions were available. This is typically not the case. Is the arms race worsening? How vulnerable are Americans to terrorist attacks? Is the quality of the environment improving? Such problems are important, but in the absence of objective, precise indicators of reality, we have no way of assessing how well they are covered. As a general matter, the less developed the system of social recording, the more likely it is that news coverage becomes a substitute for reality rather than its faithful messenger.

To develop an informed public opinion requires that television news not only allocate attention judiciously, but also interpret those events judged worthy of attention wisely. Assessing television's success in this respect is even more treacherous. Consider, for example, Braestrup's (1977/83) exhaustive examination of American media coverage of the Tet offensive in South Vietnam in 1968.[5] Braestrup claims that television news interpreted the offensive as a staggering defeat for South Vietnam and as a repudiation of President Johnson's policies. In point of fact, according to Braestrup, Tet was a military disaster and a political setback for the North, not the South. In addition, Braestrup challenges the media view that Tet demolished Johnson's pacification program. Nevertheless, it was the interpretation of Tet, not its reality, that shaped subsequent events. Portrayed as an unmitigated disaster for South Vietnam and the United States, Tet ignited a political firestorm in Washington which led to Johnson's withdrawal from the 1968 presidential contest, and generally strengthened the antiwar movement in Congress and around the country.[6]

If this example suggests the political consequences at stake in television's interpretation of reality, it also raises formidable questions about how reality is to be defined. For a description of what *really* went on during Tet, Braestrup relied on his own observations and on such sources as Oberdorfer's *Tet!* (1971) and Schandler's *The Unmaking of a President* (1977). Why should we regard these as truer accounts, somehow free from the shortcomings that, according to Braestrup, plagued television coverage in the immediate aftermath of Tet?[7]

For reasons we take to be obvious, the discussion that follows puts aside the unattainable standard of "what really happened." We do not presume to possess impeccable and authoritative accounts of reality against which to measure the performance of television news. No such standards exist—*The New York Times's* "All the News That's Fit to Print" notwithstanding.

Instead of asking whether television portrays the world accurately, we ask whether it portrays the world *differently* from other news sources. And if these are systematic differences, are they likely to en-hance or undermine an informed public opinion? To strengthen or menace representative government? In an attempt to answer these questions, we take up four possibilities. Perhaps television news con-veys representations of American society and politics that: (1) are unusually nation-centered in general and president-centered in par-ticular; (2) are posed so authoritatively as to discourage the citizen's en-gagement in national life; (3) trivialize and demean elections; and (4) undermine the authority of political institutions.

PRESIDENTIAL NEWS

Network news is national news. Compared to newspapers, which re-spond for the most part to local audiences with parochial interests, net-work news strives to attract a national audience. To do so, the networks concentrate on Washington—on the Presidency, the Congress, and the Supreme Court—and on international events that seem to impinge upon the national interest. The difference between television news and newspaper news in this respect is striking:

Network news is not simply more national in outlook, as one might expect, but is *much more* national than newspaper news . . . by a two- or three-to-one ratio over the newspapers, network television focuses its audience's interest not only on national stories but on stories that are linked to either national political figures or institutions—e.g., the activities of congressional committees, ac-tions taken by the president, or other partisan activities going on in Washing-ton (Rubin 1981, 152).[8]

If television news is unusually nation-centered, it is even more president-centered. Compared to newspaper news, television news much more often places the president at the center of things. In an examination of news coverage during 1980, for example, Robinson and Sheehan (1983) found that the CBS Evening News led off its broadcast with a story that featured the president 60 percent of the time. Natu-rally enough, if trips to Camp David and meetings with obscure ambas-sadors are covered as a matter of routine, major presidential addresses are covered lavishly. When the president speaks, the networks listen and so, therefore, do millions of Americans (Behr and Iyengar 1985). All this may enhance the president's capacity to set the public's agenda.

Or does it? There is no denying that television news is preoccupied with the president and that, in turn, the scheduling of White House activities is profoundly influenced by the tempo of television network news. The resulting attention gives the president the opportunity to focus the public's attention and to set the terms by which his performance will be judged. But while presidents certainly try to exploit this opportunity, it is not obvious how often or how completely they succeed. Presidents enjoy unparalleled access to the network's scarce air time, and they can manufacture news. However, they also have to respond to developments beyond their control. "Merchandising," as Neustadt (1960, 73) put it, perhaps a bit too confidently, "is no match for history."[9]

It may even be that television news's fixation on the president constitutes something of a threat to his public prestige. As Americans have grown more and more reliant on the networks for their news about the world, they may also have grown more president-centered in their political thinking. Thanks in part to television's fascination with the president, the American public may have developed extravagant ideas about what any president can and should do. Over the long haul, television news may contribute (if inadvertently) to the public's sense of the president's responsibilities—not in any formal, Constitutional sense, but in terms of what standards the public applies in judging presidential performance.

Consider, as one example, the case of economic performance. High unemployment, rising prices, and slow growth eat away at a president's popularity.[10] Television news certainly does not create this connection, but by placing the president at the center of public life, and particularly at the center of economic life, probably strengthens it. Thus, a president who presides over a faltering economy through no fault of his own (after all, the president is just one participant in the policy-making process [see, for example, Dahl and Lindblom 1953; Kingdon 1984]), may find his power diminished and his days in office numbered. That the public holds the president accountable for good and bad economic times testifies to the special prominence of the presidency in the American mind—and perhaps in part, to the predominance of television news in American society.

Although television news has contributed to a president-centered view of government, it could contribute to a more realistic view, one in which Congress, the bureaucracy, interest groups, and other participants get more play. In several of our experiments, people who watched news coverage of national problems that downplayed the president's responsibilities came away more likely to view these problems as significant, but *less* likely to use the problems as criteria for evaluating the president's performance. We presume that, by ignoring the president, these stories refocused attention on other actors in the political process. For the networks, watching the president is a deeply ingrained habit. Nevertheless, we would prefer to see a better and more realistic treatment of the policy-making process. Television news *could* tell a different story, one that embeds the president in a broader institutional and political framework: the presidency as a single cog in a very large machine. The public, and perhaps presidents, would be better for it.

AUTHORITATIVE NEWS

Television news is not only distinctive in its focus—its preoccupation with the nation and especially the president—but also in its presentation. Television news is news without ambiguity, equivocation, or uncertainty. It is, or poses as, *authoritative* news. P. H. Weaver argues, in a stylish and provocative dissection of the differences between television news and newspaper news: "There is hardly an aspect of the scripting, casting, and staging of a television news program that is not designed to convey an impression of authority and omniscience. This can be seen most strikingly in the role of the anchorman—Walter Cronkite is the exemplar—who is positively god-like: he summons forth men, events, and images at will; he speaks in tones of utter certainty; he is the person with whom all things begin and end" (1975, 84). This mantle of authority extends as well to the television reporter in the field who typically towers over the scene in question and who "speaks authoritatively and self-confidently about everything that comes into his field of vision: men, events, motives, intentions, meanings, significances, trends, threats, problems, solutions—all are evidently within his perfect understanding, and he pronounces on them without any ifs, ands, or buts" (Weaver 1975, 90).

Most Americans, most of the time, seem to find this authoritative pose irresistible. According to various national surveys, Americans believe by a wide margin that television—not magazines, radio, or newspapers—provides the most intelligent, complete, and impartial news coverage (Bower 1985). In a national survey carried out in June of 1984, 79 percent of the American public expressed approval of how the networks handle the job of reporting the news.[11] While the public's confidence in many national institutions has been eroding, faith in television news has actually been increasing (Bower 1985). It could be that such faith is well-deserved: perhaps television news has earned public confidence through its excellent coverage and penetrating analysis. Perhaps. We suspect, however, that such faith is founded on the pose and pretense of authority. Americans trust the evening news more than they should.[12]

One regrettable and quite unintended consequence of television's special style of presentation may be to discourage active and critical participation in political life. Television news presents interpretations with great confidence, almost as if they were embedded in the events themselves and therefore not open to question: "CBS speaks to the audience as a provider of authoritative information. It solicits nothing beyond their attention, solicits of them no active role vis-à-vis the political material reported: indeed the authoritative and detached style of the report and the finality of the sign-off leave the impression that the matters discussed are essentially closed, at least until the next broadcast" (Hallin 1985, 135). In addition, television news often insinuates that politics belongs to a sphere that includes journalists as well as other political elites, but excludes the audience (Hallin and Mancini 1984). With its authoritative trappings, television news seems to be saying that ordinary people cannot manage politics and should not try, that politics is for and about elites, not for and about the viewer. In this respect, television news is profoundly antidemocratic.

SUPERFICIAL NEWS

A third possible aspect of television's distinctiveness is superficiality. Patterson and McClure (1976) have argued that television news promotes a superficial view of campaigns and elections, thereby cultivating contempt for the democratic process. In particular, they complain that the networks degrade presidential elections by portraying them as little more than grand sporting events. Instead of covering the serious matters of policy and qualifications, the networks "devote most of their election coverage to the trivia of political campaigning that make for flashy pictures. Hecklers, crowds, motorcades, balloons, rallies and gossip—these are the regular subjects of network campaign stories" (Patterson and McClure, 22). The discouraging result is a "television audience obsessed with election nonsense. What the viewer watches— the campaign trivia the networks so prominently display—is precisely how the viewer describes and defines the election world he cannot see with his own eyes" (Patterson and McClure, 76).

Television news does indeed pay relatively little attention to policy in its coverage of presidential campaigns and a great deal of attention to the dynamics of the contest itself—with who is ahead and why.[13] But it is not at all clear that television news should be singled out for special criticism in this regard. The networks appear to be no more preoccupied with winning and losing, with campaign strategy and hoopla, than are the daily newspapers, national weekly newsmagazines, or the wire services. Indeed, some results show that television news is *less* preoccupied with such matters (Robinson and Sheehan 1983). Moreover, the superficial coverage of presidential campaigns that Patterson and McClure deplore was not exactly invented by television. Lazarsfeld, Berelson, and Gaudet's (1948) careful analysis of coverage of the 1940 presidential campaign echoes contemporary results with near perfect fidelity. And finally, that presidential campaigns are seldom portrayed as clashes over policy may have a good bit to do with the campaign events themselves: candidates' discussion of their policy positions usually plays a modest role in the typical presidential campaign (Page 1978; Arterton 1984). No news medium can be expected to cover a campaign that never was.

In short, preoccupation with winning and losing is not the special province of television. This preoccupation is characteristic of American journalism in general, a reflection of a theory of politics that is widely shared among members of the American press. The core of the theory has been well-described by Weaver:

Politics is essentially a game played by individual politicians for personal advancement, gain or power. The game is a competitive one, and the players' principal activities are those of calculating and pursuing strategies designed to defeat competitors and to achieve their goals (usually election to public office). Of course, the game takes place against a backdrop of governmental institutions, public problems, policy debates, and the like, but these are noteworthy only insofar as they affect, or are used by, players in pursuit of the game's rewards (1972, 69).

Because strategy and calculation lie at the heart of the journalist's theory, so, too, do strategy and calculation lie at the heart of the typical campaign story. Witness, for example, the extraordinary attention conferred upon the first tests of the candidates' prospects—in recent contests, the Iowa caucuses, and the New Hampshire primaries. Statements of policy, rarely prominent in the campaign anyway, are accorded attention only insofar as they seem to bear on the changing fortunes of the candidates. The networks devoted sustained coverage to George McGovern's ill-fated income redistribution proposal in 1972, Ronald Reagan's opposition to the Panama Canal treaty in 1976, and Walter Mondale's dramatic tax increase announcement in 1984 because these policy positions were expected to have strategic significance. Such proposals were treated less as opportunities to explore the candidate's philosophy of government and more as potential strategic miscalculations that might diminish the candidate's support (Matthews 1978). This emphasis on the strategic side of campaigns is nowhere more evident than in coverage of the occasional presidential debates. Although the debates are typically crammed with facts, policies, and programs, postdebate coverage has typically concentrated on who won, how each side had prepared, and what the ramifications appear to be for each side's chances (e.g., Sears and Chaffee 1979).

We object to the one-dimensional nature of campaign coverage. It is true that candidates often behave as if they wanted nothing else in the world except to be elected (or returned) to office (Mayhew 1974). However, campaigns and elections are not merely personal quests for power, but also concern the distribution of power in society, the resolution or exacerbation of conflict, and the ascendancy of certain values and interests over others. To ignore these alternative perspectives on politics is to diminish voters' comprehension of the choices they confront.

As would be expected from our results on priming, when campaign coverage is preoccupied with winning and losing, so, too, are voters. Early in the presidential primary season, the choices voters make are powerfully influenced by their sense of which candidates have a chance to win—something they can pick up easily, almost automatically, from television, newspapers, and magazines (Bartels 1985). If the *only* story is the campaign, then practically all voters, no matter how involved they may be with other matters, will know who is ahead and who is behind. Such relentless promotion of a single view of the campaign reduces the electorate's capacity to choose wisely.

Remedies? We would like to see multiple portrayals of campaigns, each a reflection of a different point of view on the nature of politics. This would seem to require, to borrow Weaver's phrase, "an enlargement of the journalistic imagination and an expansion of the journalist's vision" (1972, 74). We say this wistfully, with no expectation that it will happen soon.

OPPOSITIONAL NEWS

Finally, some have argued that television news is distinctive in the adversarial stance it assumes toward political authority. This view has been championed most aggressively by Robinson (1976a, 1976b, 1977), who traced Americans' diminishing confidence in national political institutions through the 1960s and 1970s to their growing reliance on television news, which he characterized as "inferential, dramatic, negativistic, contentious, and disestablishmentarian" (1976a, 427). Robinson concluded that it was television news—rather than the political events of the period—that led us to question and doubt our political institutions. This political disaffection he termed "videomalaise."

Robinson's diagnosis proved popular. To Huntington (1975), for example, television news in the 1960s was a "dispatriating" agency; by constantly conveying the impression that things were falling apart, television news was eating away at the authority of political institutions. In the same vein, Rothman (1980) complained that television news was cultivating an ideology of despair by portraying institutions as corrupt, modern technology as dangerous, political discontent and social disorganization as signs of impending catastrophic social collapse, and countercultural escapades as healthy reactions to a sick society. Finally, in *Channels of Power*, Ranney (1983) argued that television news "has altered the culture significantly by intensifying ordinary Americans' traditional low opinion of politics and politicians, by exacerbating the decline in their trust and confidence in the government and its institutions, and by helping to make them even less inclined to vote than they used to be" (86–87).[14]

These accusations are strong, but the evidence is weak. The empirical base for the claim that television news induces malaise consists of just two results. The first is Robinson's (1976a) finding that citizens who rely primarily on television for news about politics tend to be more cynical about the motives and capabilities of public officials and more skeptical of their own ability to influence government than are those who draw on other sources for their political news. This correlation is consistent with the videomalaise hypothesis, but subsequent research has failed to corroborate it. Indeed, with improved measures and better analysis, the relationship between television dependence and political disaffection disappears (Miller, Goldenberg, and Erbring 1980). The second result comes from an experiment, in which ordinary midwesterners were or were not induced to watch the CBS documentary "The Selling of the Pentagon," and then questioned about their political views (Robinson 1976a). The point of the documentary was that the Pentagon was spending millions of dollars each year on elaborate marketing and advertising schemes, all designed to build support for its programs and budget. It seems quite reasonable to us for citizens to conclude after an hour's worth of revelations of huge shenanigans in high places that politics is complicated. And this is precisely what Robinson found. Immediately after the presentation, viewers of the documentary expressed less confidence in their ability to understand politics, were more likely to believe that the Pentagon lobbies on its own behalf, and were less likely to believe that the military stays out of politics. However, viewers of the documentary did *not* become more negative toward the Department of Defense or toward the military in general. Consequently, we see little in these results to support the sweeping claim of videomalaise.[15] And this leaves us unpersuaded by Huntington, Rothman, or Ranney, since virtually the only evidence they cite is Robinson's.

Moreover, the very premise that television serves as an oppositional force seems to us inaccurate. The oppositional thesis certainly collides with what we know about television coverage of presidential campaigns. Despite sometimes sharp differences in method, the same findings of cautious and overwhelming objectivity show up in study after study. As a general rule, reporters merely provide accounts of the day's events; they do not interject their own views. Of course, not all stories follow this script, and there is a hint that these rare excursions into subjective political analysis and judgment tend to be negative more often on the television screen than on the front page. But the available evidence indicates that such differences are modest; more often there are no differences at all.[16] This evidence is hard to square with the view of television news as an oppositional force.

The evidence testifies instead to the American media's deep commitment to "objectivity." As a professional ideology, objectivity includes three commitments: to independence (journalism should be free from political pressures); to balance (journalism should present without favor the positions of all contending parties); and to objectivity (journalism should simply present the facts, without passing judgment on them). These ideological commitments have become intertwined over the last several decades with a set of working routines that have promoted the development of intimate relationships between members of the press and members of the government. Journalists have increasingly come to rely on government officials and agencies as their primary source of information, and to focus on their activities as the basic subject matter of news. Government officials, for their part, need journalists to communicate both with the public and with other elites.[17]

Coverage of presidential campaigns incorporates these elements of objectivity well. Campaign news is first and foremost official news: it pays great attention to the contestants and rather less to what the consequences of the election might be for the public. Campaign news also appears free from the most vulgar political pressures, is balanced at least in the sense of giving equal time to the "serious" candidates and, for the most part, simply relays factual accounts of the day's events. Television coverage of presidential campaigns is objective news, not oppositional news.

Objective journalism also seems to have prevailed in television coverage of the Vietnam War. This conclusion is important, because those who see television news as an oppositional force often point to coverage of the war as providing decisive evidence in support of their case. The conclusion may also be surprising. Network coverage of the war did change after the Tet offensive in early 1968, becoming more critical of the Johnson administration's policies, the South Vietnamese regime, and the military efforts of the American and South Vietnamese troops (Hallin 1986; also see Braestrup 1977/83). Moreover, such changes in coverage seemed to outstrip the changes actually taking place in Vietnam, a pattern that is consistent with the oppositional thesis.

A close look at television coverage, however, indicates that the ideology of objective journalism was in fact preserved throughout this turbulent period. Television's treatment of the war became more critical after Tet only as visible and legitimate political elites became outspoken in their dissent from the administration's policies. That is, television took its cues once again from official sources, this time duly reporting the collapse of consensus within Washington elites. While coverage of the president's critics did increase after Tet, such coverage was not particularly positive, and was flatly negative toward those unruly types who, in the language of the times, worked "outside the system" (Hallin 1984; Gitlin 1980). Stories that questioned official sources were exceedingly rare, even after Tet. According to Hallin's (1984) analysis, Americans who sat glued to their television screens night after night would have witnessed about one such story each *month*. If Vietnam constitutes a decisive case for the oppositional thesis, the oppositional thesis is in deep trouble. The results indicate instead the reign of objectivity.

That television news is politically objective does not mean that television news is politically neutral. If the politics of television news are difficult to see, it is partly because they are so familiar and comfortable. Without having good evidence in hand, it seems to us that television news, and American news in general, reflects and sustains a set of traditional American values. Television news glorifies democracy, especially the romantic town hall variety; condemns demagogues, bureaucracies, political "machines," and movements of the extreme left or right; celebrates capitalism and individualism; and reveres the existing social order (Gans 1979). At the same time, television news, and American news in general, reflects and sustains the "official" view. Journalists rely heavily on officials and on routine channels of information—the press conference, the informal briefing, and the handout—in order to remain true to their ideology of objectivity and to cope with the complexity of their jobs. But in so doing, they leave much of the task of defining what news is to officials. The danger, of course, is that journalists become "mere stenographers for the official transcript of social reality" (Schudson 1978, 185), while the networks and the newspapers become "house organs for the political elite" (Sigal 1973, 47).[18]

We believe these values and routines shape the pictures and stories that appear on the news each evening, as some events are transformed into news and, more to the point, some are ignored. The doctrine of objectivity frequently means that candidates and groups with exotic points of view get no play (Robinson and Sheehan 1983) or, if they are covered at all, the point of the news story is to reveal how odd they are, not what they have to say (Gitlin 1980). Moreover, with respect to those matters that Lindblom has called "the grand issues of politico-economic organization: private enterprise, a high degree of corporate autonomy, protection of the status quo on distribution of income and wealth, close consultation between business and government, and restriction of union demands to those consistent with business profitability" (1977, 205), there is mainly dead silence.

Television news may be objective, but it is far from neutral. The production of news takes place within boundaries established by official sources and dominant values. To regard television news as a "never-tiring political opposition, a maverick third party which never need face the sobering experience of governing" (Robinson 1976, 126) seems to us quite misleading. Instead, we see television news as an inherently cautious and conservative medium, much more likely to defend traditional values and institutions than to attack them.

Because television now fits so comfortably and naturally into our lives, it is easy to take for granted: "We are no longer fascinated or perplexed by its machinery. We do not tell stories of its wonders. We do not confine our television sets to special rooms. We do not doubt the reality of what we see on television, are largely unaware of the special angle of vision it affords" (Postman 1985, 79). This sleepy acquiescence may be hazardous to our political health. Moreover, just as television should not be taken for granted, it cannot be dismissed merely because so much of it is awful. Much of it—including television news programming—*is* awful. But that judgment does not alter the overwhelming fact that, for good or ill, television has become a mature and powerful force in American politics. In commanding attention and shaping opinion, television is now an authority virtually without peer. Near the close of the twentieth century, in the shadow of Orwell's *1984*, it would be both naive and irresponsible to pretend that such an authority could ever be neutral.

Appendixes

Appendix A
Summary of Experiments

Experiment	Date	Location*	Design**	Target Problem(s)	Factor(s) Manipulated	Number of Treatment Groups	Number of Participants
1	11/80	NH	S	Defense	Amount of coverage	2	28
2	2/81	NH	S	Defense Inflation Pollution	Amount of coverage	3	44
3	4–5/81	NH	A	Energy	Amount of coverage; Degree of presidential responsibility	5	73†
4	5–6/81	NH	A	Energy Defense Inflation	Amount of coverage; Degree of presidential responsibility	12	140
5	8–9/81	NH	A	Social security Civil rights Unemployment	Amount of coverage; Personal relevance	6	110
6	11–12/81	NH	A	Unemployment Pollution	Amount of coverage; Vivid vs. pallid coverage	8	104

	Date			Topic	Variable		
7	6/82	NH	A	Hostage crisis Camp David	Amount of coverage; Good vs. bad news	5	64
8	7/82	NH	S	Unemployment Arms control Civil rights	Amount of coverage	3	63
9	8/82	NH	S	Unemployment	Amount of coverage; Personal relevance	4	68
10	10/82	NH	S	Economy Candidate qualities	Amount of coverage	3	56
11 ††	5/83	AA	A	Unemployment	Vivid vs. pallid presentation	3	58
12	5/83	AA	A	Unemployment Energy	Presidential responsibility	6	136
13	6/83	AA	A	Unemployment Energy	Presidential responsibility	4	86
14	8/83	NH	A	Illegal drugs Education	Amount of coverage; Lead story vs. middle story	4	121

* NH = New Haven, Connecticut; AA = Ann Arbor, Michigan
** S = Sequential Design; A = Assemblage Design
† Yale University undergraduates
†† University of Michigan undergraduates

CHAPTER 3

TIME-SERIES ANALYSIS OF AGENDA-SETTING

No single survey organization regularly used the question "What do you think is the most important problem facing the nation?" We therefore relied on three different organizations: American Institute of Public Opinion (AIPO), Yankelovich, and the Center for Political Studies (CPS) of the University of Michigan. Using all three, we were able to obtain a reading for every two-month period between 1974 and 1980, except three. We estimated the three missing observations through interpolation.

In their original condition, the data from the three organizations were not fully comparable. Both AIPO and Yankelovich accept multiple answers, while CPS does not. In addition, Yankelovich consistently records a larger number of responses than does AIPO. Thus in any given month Yankelovich generally reports the highest percentage of respondents citing a given problem while CPS reports the lowest.

Instead of relying on the percentage of respondents, we calculated the percentage of *responses* concerning each problem. This transformation yielded essentially equivalent readings for the several months in which more than one of the survey organizations asked the question. For instance, in August 1979, both AIPO and Yankelovich asked about the most important problem facing the nation. Among AIPO respondents, 20 percent cited energy, 8 percent cited unemployment, and 50 percent mentioned inflation. In contrast, among respondents surveyed by Yankelovich, 35 percent listed energy, 10 percent named unemployment, and 81 percent cited inflation. These figures, based on percentages of *respondents*, are clearly inconsistent. However, when the percentages of *responses* are calculated, the inconsistency disappears. The figures for AIPO are then 15 percent for energy, 6 percent for unemployment, and 39 percent for inflation, while for Yankelovich they are 18 percent for energy, 5 percent for unemployment, and 44 percent for inflation. On the basis of several such comparisons, we concluded that calculating the percentage of responses allowed us to use the three different surveys interchangeably.

In the various two-month periods when the "most important problem" question was included in more than one poll, either by the same or by different organizations, the surveys were pooled, and then the percent of responses expressing concern with each problem was tabulated.

The following surveys were used: AIPO 886, 906, 913, 915, 916, 924, 932, 938, 943, 950, 960, 961, 970, 980, 986, 993, 999, 1106, 1111, 1123, 1128, 1136, 1141, 1151, 1157, 1159, and 1162; Yankelovich 8400, 8422, 8430, 8440, 8460, 8510, 8520, 8530, 8550, 8105, 8117, 8125, 8149, 8156, 8161, 8181, 8182, 8184, and 8260; CPS National Election Surveys for 1972, 1976, and 1978.

The subject matter of presidential speeches was determined from *Vital Speeches* (City News Pub. Co., N.Y.). Speeches were classified according to their primary emphasis. Only addresses to the nation were coded. Presidential speeches on energy occurred on: 18 April 1977; 8 November 1977; 19 January 1978; 15 April 1979; 15 July 1979; and 14 March 1980. Speeches on unemployment occurred on: 15 January 1974; 19 January 1976; 12 January 1977; 2 February 1977; and 19 January 1978. Speeches on inflation occurred on: 25 July 1974; 12 August 1974; 24 October 1978; 23 January 1979; and 14 March 1980.

Meetings of OPEC ministers were also coded. The dates of these meetings were: 19 January 1974; 13 September 1974; 13 December 1974; 5 March 1975; 10 June 1975; 28 September 1975; 20 December 1975; 26 May 1976; 15 December 1976; 19 December 1977; 19 June 1978; 15 December 1978; 26 March 1979; 27 June 1979; 17 December 1979; 6 May 1980; 9 June 1980; 16 September 1980; and 15 December 1980.

Measures of inflation and unemployment were taken from the Council of Economic Advisors' *Monthly Economic Reports*. These included the national unemployment rate, the average duration of unemployment, the consumer price index, the consumer price index for food, and the average rate of interest on consumer loans. The energy measures were coded from the Department of Energy's *Monthly Energy Review*. These included the consumer price index for energy, the price index for home heating oil, the price index for gasoline, and the amount of imported petroleum stocks.

The analysis proceeded in two separate stages. In the first stage, we estimated the effects of real world conditions, public opinion, and presidential speeches on news coverage for each of the three problems separately. In the second stage, we estimated the effects of news coverage, real world conditions, and presidential speeches on the percentage of public responses naming inflation, energy, or unemployment as the most important problem facing the nation. In equation form:

(3.1)   TV news $= \beta_0 + \beta_1$ real world $+ \beta_2$ public concern $+ \beta_3$ presidential speeches $+ \varepsilon_1$

(3.2)   Public concern $= \beta_0 + \beta_1$ real world $+ \beta_2$ TV news $+ \beta_3$ presidential speeches $+ \varepsilon_2$

Equations 3.1 and 3.2 represent the structural relationship of interest. In addition, because of the transformations required to make the data from the three polling organizations comparable, responses citing one problem necessarily cause the percentage of responses referring to other problems to decrease. To adjust for this relationship, each equation also includes the percentage of responses citing the other two problems.

In order to estimate each of the six equations in the model (a pair of equations for each of three problems), there must be at least five variables excluded from each equation. We met this requirement; all our equations are identified. (For details, consult Behr and Iyengar 1985.)

To correct for problems of simultaneity and positive autocorrelation, we use the maximum likelihood, simultaneous equations estimator developed by Fair (1970). When only autocorrelation is a problem, we use a simple maximum likelihood estimator (see Johnston 1972). Finally, when only simultaneity exists, we use two-stage least squares.

In each of the three second stage equations, the key coefficient is β_2. A positively signed and statistically significant β_2 means that increases in television news coverage of a particular problem lead to increases in the importance ascribed to that problem by the public, consistent with the agenda-setting hypothesis. This coefficient is the independent effect of news coverage on public opinion controlling for actual conditions, presidential speeches, and the feedback effect of public opinion on news coverage.

CHAPTER 4

TIME-SERIES ESTIMATES OF THE EFFECTS OF LEAD STORIES

The separate effects of lead stories and nonlead stories were estimated by including the number of both types of stories devoted to each of the three problems under study as right-hand variables in the public concern equation (3.2 above). Both were treated as endogenous predictors. The estimated coefficients are given below.

Determinants of Public Opinion toward Energy, Inflation and Unemployment:
January 1974–December 1980

	Energy	Inflation	Unemployment
Lead Stories	1.06	.83	.31
	(.31)	(.46)	(1.03)
Nonlead Stories	.10	.03	.09
	(.15)	(.19)	(.35)

Note: Table entries are two-stage, maximum likelihood coefficients (col. 1), o.l.s. coefficients (col. 2) or maximum likelihood coefficients (col. 3), with estimated standard errors in parentheses.

CHAPTER 5

In the first analysis reported below, employment status was represented by a single dichotomous variable: respondents who were currently unemployed at the time of the interview were coded "1"; all others were coded "0." In the second analysis reported below, employment status was represented by a series of dichotomous variables: currently employed vs. not; currently temporarily laid off vs. not; currently working now but either worried about the future or had problems in the past vs. not; and retired, disabled, housewives, students vs. not. The implicit reference group for this series is made up of those currently employed with no worries about the future and no problems in the past.

Determinants of Most Important Problem Mentions I: 1980, 1982 National Election
Studies Pooled

Variable	Equation		
	(1) Civil Rights	(2) Unemployment	(3) Social Security
Race	1.466	.444	.349
	(.516)	(.128)	(.178)
Employment status	−.619	.436	−.500
	(.785)	(.167)	(.224)
Age	.117	−.136	.186
	(.144)	(.024)	(.036)
Year	−.416	.915	1.454
	(.497)	(.082)	(.142)
Constant	−5.427	−1.025	−4.364
	(1.864)	(.386)	(.554)

Note: Number of respondents = 2706.
Table entries are probit coefficients with standard errors in parentheses.

Determinants of Most Important Problem Mentions II: 1980, 1982 National Election
Studies Pooled

	Equation		
Variable	(1) Civil Rights	(2) Unemployment	(3) Social Security
Race	1.430 (.519)	.426 (.129)	.328 (.179)
Unemployed	.887 (.864)	.500 (.183)	.691 (.246)
Temporarily laid off	−3.301 (17.497)	1.240 (.512)	−.577 (1.043)
Working now but wor- ried about future or problems in the past	.746 (.621)	.330 (.109)	.120 (.174)
Retired, disabled, stu- dents, housewives, not working	−.605 (.725)	.159 (.104)	.226 (.158)
Age	.252 (.169)	−.134 (.027)	.159 (.040)
Year	−.486 (.499)	.902 (.083)	1.443 (.142)
Constant	−4.718 (17.683)	−4.233 (.665)	−5.832 (1.244)

Note: Number of respondents = 2708.
Table entries are probit coefficients with standard errors in parentheses.

Chapter 6

To test whether different types of viewers are differentially susceptible
to agenda-setting, we combined experiments 2, 8, and 9 and estimated
the following equation:

(6.1)   Postexperimental importance =
         $\beta_0 + \beta_1$ preexperimental importance + β_2 viewer type + ε

In this equation, change is defined as the difference between the
importance viewers assigned to the target problem at the conclusion of
the experiment and the importance predicted by the viewers' preexperimental beliefs. Viewers whose actual postexperimental judgments
exceeded the predicted judgments changed to a greater degree than
did viewers whose actual postexperimental judgments fell below the
predicted judgments. The interesting question is then whether different types of viewers show more or less change, where viewer type is

defined by education, partisanship, and political involvement. The equation takes up each of these in turn.

Experiments 2, 8, and 9 measure problem importance both through composite ratings and spontaneous mentions. We estimated equation 6.1 somewhat differently in the two cases. In the first, we treated viewers' composite ratings offered before the experiment began as an endogenous variable and employed two-stage least squares to produce consistent estimates of the coefficients (Johnston 1972). We would have preferred to follow this same procedure for the spontaneous mentions, but we could not. The two-stage procedure requires the specification of instrumental variables for the first stage equations—in this case, variables that affect viewers' preexperimental judgments but not directly their postexperimental judgments. We were able to locate such

Change in Problem Importance Among Different Types of Viewers: Experiments 2, 8, and 9 Combined (Multivariate Analysis)

	Composite Ratings*	Spontaneous Mention**
Preexperimental Score		
	.77	3.88
	(.09)	(.70)
Education		
High school or less	.30	—
	(.28)	
Party Identification		
Independents	.39	—
	(.27)	
Republicans	—	−1.15
		(.78)
Involvement		
Follows public affairs rarely	.39	.77
	(.26)	(.49)
Pays little attention to news- paper coverage of politics	—	—
Doesn't read a daily newspaper	—	—
Watches the news rarely	.51	—
	(.20)	
Discusses politics rarely	.38	.84
	(.32)	(.50)
Politically inactive	.20	.24
	(.12)	(.19)
No expertise	—	—

*2SLS coefficients, with estimated standard errors in parentheses. For the overall equation, adjusted $R^2 = .72$, standard error = 1.47.

**Logit coefficients, with estimated standard errors in parentheses. For the overall equation, alternative $R^2 = .80$, log likelihood ratio = −52.40, Chi-square = 67.60.

variables in the case of composite ratings (R-squared for the first-stage equation = .23), but not in the case of spontaneous mentions. As a consequence, the coefficients reported in table 6.1 are based directly on equation 6.1, estimated through the maximum likelihood logit procedure appropriate for dichotomous dependent variables (Hanushek and Jackson 1977).

The results of the multivariate analysis are provided on the previous page. That analysis follows the logic described so far, except that the effects of the various viewer characteristics are considered all at once. A blank cell in the table means that the coefficient was omitted from the final equation, based on interim results.

Chapter 7

ESTIMATING PRIMING

Experiment 1. In formal terms, we tested the priming hypothesis in experiment 1 by estimating the following equation:

(7.1)   General performance = $\beta_0 + \beta_1$ (defense performance)
   $+ \beta_2$ (defense performance $\times$ treatment) $+ \varepsilon$

$$\text{where Treatment} = \begin{cases} 1 \text{ for viewers in defense condition,} \\ 0 \text{ for viewers in control condition.} \end{cases}$$

The priming hypothesis is tested in equation 7.1 by β_2. This parameter estimates the additional impact of defense performance ratings on overall evaluations, that results from exposure to news about defense. A statistically significant and positively signed β_2 means that news coverage of defense increased the weight viewers granted to President Carter's performance on defense in their overall evaluations of the President. Unless explicitly noted otherwise, here and elsewhere, parameters were estimated by ordinary least squares regression.

Technically, equation 7.1 and those that follow should include *all* lower-order terms implied by higher-order interactions. In the particular case of equation 7.1, this would mean including terms for the main effects of treatment. In fact, in initial runs, we did include all the implied lower-order terms in each of the equations we estimated. The coefficients associated with these lower-order terms generally did not stray from zero, however. Where they were indistinguishable from zero, they were deleted from the equations reported here.

Experiment 2.

(7.2)   General performance = $\beta_0 + \beta_1$ (defense performance)
   $+ \beta_2$ (inflation performance) $+$

β_3 (defense performance $\times$ treatment$_1$) +
β_4 (inflation performance $\times$ treatment$_2$) + ε

$$\text{where Treatment}_1 = \begin{cases} 1 \text{ for viewers in defense condition,} \\ 0 \text{ for viewers in inflation condition;} \end{cases}$$

$$\text{Treatment}_2 = \begin{cases} 1 \text{ for viewers in inflation condition,} \\ 0 \text{ for viewers in defense condition.} \end{cases}$$

β_1 and β_2 are the baseline impacts of problem performance. β_3 and β_4 test the priming hypothesis associated with news coverage of defense and inflation respectively. A positively signed and statistically significant β_3 indicates that exposure to stories about defense elevates the importance of defense in overall evaluations of the president's performance, in keeping with the priming hypothesis. A statistically significant and positively signed β_4 indicates the same for inflation.

Experiment 9.

(7.3)   General performance = $\beta_0 + \beta_1$ (unemployment performance)
+ β_2 (unemployment performance $\times$ treatment) + ε

$$\text{where Treatment} = \begin{cases} 1 \text{ for viewers who watched unemploy-} \\ \text{ment newscasts,} \\ 0 \text{ otherwise.} \end{cases}$$

A positively signed and statistically significant β_2 indicates that exposure to stories about unemployment elevates the importance of unemployment in overall evaluations of the president's performance, in keeping with the priming hypothesis.

Experiment 8.

(7.4)   General performance = $\beta_0 + \beta_1$ (arms control performance)
+ β_2 (civil rights performance)
+ β_3 (unemployment performance)
+ β_4 (arms control performance $\times$ treatment$_1$)
+ β_5 (civil rights performance $\times$ treatment$_2$)
+ β_6 (unemployment performance $\times$ treatment$_3$) + ε

$$\text{where Treatment}_1 = \begin{cases} 1 \text{ for viewers in arms control} \\ \text{treatment,} \\ 0 \text{ otherwise;} \end{cases}$$

$$\text{Treatment}_2 = \begin{cases} 1 \text{ for viewers in civil rights treatment,} \\ 0 \text{ otherwise;} \end{cases}$$

$$\text{Treatment}_3 = \begin{cases} 1 \text{ for viewers in unemployment} \\ \text{treatment,} \\ 0 \text{ otherwise.} \end{cases}$$

Baseline effects are tested by β_1, β_2, β_3. Priming effects are tested by β_4, β_5, and β_6.

Experiments 3 and 4.

(7.5) General performance = $\beta_0 + \beta_1$ (energy performance)
$+ \beta_2$ (energy performance $\times$ treatment) $+ \varepsilon$

$$\text{where Treatment} = \begin{cases} 1 \text{ for viewers who saw several or many} \\ \text{energy stories,} \\ 0 \text{ for viewers who saw no energy stories.} \end{cases}$$

(7.6) General performance = $\beta_0 + \beta_1$ (energy performance)
$+ \beta_2$ (energy performance $\times$ treatment$_1$)
$+ \beta_3$ (defense performance)
$+ \beta_4$ (defense performance $\times$ treatment$_2$)
$+ \beta_5$ (inflation performance)
$+ \beta_6$ (inflation performance $\times$ treatment$_3$) $+ \varepsilon$

$$\text{where Treatment}_1 = \begin{cases} 1 \text{ for viewers who saw several or many} \\ \text{energy stories,} \\ 0 \text{ otherwise;} \end{cases}$$

$$\text{Treatment}_2 = \begin{cases} 1 \text{ for viewers who saw several or many} \\ \text{defense stories,} \\ 0 \text{ otherwise;} \end{cases}$$

$$\text{Treatment}_3 = \begin{cases} 1 \text{ for viewers who saw several or many} \\ \text{inflation stories,} \\ 0 \text{ otherwise.} \end{cases}$$

Experiment 8 revisited (2SLS). We estimated priming effects purged of projection with two-stage least squares (Johnston 1972), under several different specifications. In each, judgments of the president's general performance and ratings of his performance in specific domains, both assessed in the postexperiment questionnaire, were treated as endogenous. Three variables served as instruments, all taken from the preexperimental questionnaire: ratings of the president's performance on the problem under investigation (e.g., arms control); composite ratings of the problem's importance; and open-ended mention of the problem. Specifications varied according to what other variables (all treated as exogenous, all taken from the preexperimental questionnaire) were also included in the priming equations. The first (1) included overall judgments of the president's general performance, liberalism-conservatism, and race; the second (2) included overall judgments of the president's general performance and liberalism-conservatism; and the third (3) included only overall judgments of the president's general performance. For illustrative purposes, some of these results are given below:

Priming with Projection Controlled: Estimated Impact of Arms Control Performance Ratings on Evaluations of President Reagan's General Performance

Equation	(1)	(2)	(3)
Baseline impact of arms control performance rating	.02	−.02	.05
Added impact due to priming	.58*	.76*	.69*

*$p < .05$

Chapter 8

1980 national election study (nes)

The factor analysis reported in table 8.1 was based on three independent national samples, each part of the 1980 NES: the January–February survey ($n = 1008$), undertaken after the Iowa Caucus and completed prior to the New Hampshire Primary; the April survey ($n = 965$), conducted in the window between major primaries (i.e., after Illinois and New York and before Pennsylvania and Texas), and the September–October survey ($n = 1614$), completed as the presidential campaign neared its end.

For Carter and Reagan separately, two factors were extracted from Pearson correlation matrices and then subjected to oblique rotation. (We expected distinct but *correlated* competence and integrity factors.) Table 8.1 presents the factor loadings averaged across the three surveys. This unusual aggregating procedure is faithful to each survey-specific analysis, since factor solutions were highly robust across the three surveys.

To test the gradient hypothesis, we estimated the following equation for each of the three dependent measures (overall performance, competence, and integrity):

(8.1)   Overall evaluation $= \beta_0 + \beta_1$ (inflation performance) $+$
β_2 (energy performance) $+ \beta_3$ (unemployment performance) $+$
β_4 (hostage crisis performance) $+ \beta_5$ (Afghanistan performance) $+ \varepsilon$

With the September cross-section survey, parameters were estimated
by ordinary least squares. With the September–October panel, parameters were estimated by two-stage least squares. In this case, overall evaluations and problem performance ratings were treated as endogenous. These coefficients are therefore purged of any effects due to
projection. The instruments were lagged versions of the identical variables, taken from the June interview.

1982 NATIONAL ELECTION STUDY (NES)

Following the procedure used in the 1980 cross-section survey, we estimated the following equation three times (for overall performance,
competence, and integrity):

(8.2)   Overall evaluation $= \beta_0 + \beta_1$ (arms control performance)
$+ \beta_2$ (unemployment performance) $+ \beta_3$ (defense performance)
$+ \beta_4$ (inflation performance) $+ \varepsilon$

All parameters were estimated by ordinary least squares.

CHAPTER 9

Experiment 3. To test the responsibility hypothesis in experiment 3,
we estimated the following equation:

(9.1)   Overall performance $= \beta_0 + \beta_1$ (energy performance) $+$
β_2 (energy performance $\times$ treatment) $+$
β_3 (energy performance $\times$ responsibility) $+$
β_4 (energy performance $\times$ exposure) $+ \varepsilon$

where Treatment $= \begin{cases} 1 \text{ for viewers in treatment conditions,} \\ 0 \text{ for viewers in control conditions;} \end{cases}$

Responsibility $= \begin{cases} 1 \text{ for viewers in high responsibility} \\ \text{conditions,} \\ 0 \text{ otherwise;} \end{cases}$

Exposure $= \begin{cases} 1 \text{ for viewers in high exposure} \\ \text{conditions,} \\ 0 \text{ otherwise.} \end{cases}$

As in previous equations, β_1 estimates the baseline relationship between students' assessments of Carter's success at handling energy matters and their summary ratings of him, and β_2 once again assesses the priming effect associated with the difference between no exposure to energy stories and some exposure. What is new in equation 9.1 is the effect associated with β_3, which assesses the increase in the priming due to responsibility. A statistically significant and positively signed β_3 means that stories which portray the president as responsible for energy problems exercise more influence on evaluational standards than do stories that do not so portray the president. (And for the sake of completeness and control, β_4 represents whatever evaluational impact is due to being exposed to many energy stories rather than to a few.)

Experiment 4. Testing the responsibility hypothesis in experiment 4 is somewhat more complex, since the experiment manipulates coverage of three problems, not one:

(9.2)   Overall performance $= \beta_0 + \beta_1$ (energy performance) $+$
β_2 (inflation performance) $+ \beta_3$ (defense performance) $+$
β_4 (energy performance $\times$ treatment$_1$) $+$
β_5 (inflation performance $\times$ treatment$_2$) $+$
β_6 (defense performance $\times$ treatment$_3$) $+$
β_7 (energy performance $\times$ responsibility$_1$) $+$
β_8 (inflation performance $\times$ responsibility$_2$) $+$
β_9 (defense performance $\times$ responsibility$_3$) $+$
β_{10} (energy performance $\times$ exposure$_1$) $+$
β_{11} (inflation performance $\times$ exposure$_2$) $+$
β_{12} (defense performance $\times$ exposure$_3$) $+ \varepsilon$

where Treatment$_1 = \begin{cases} 1 \text{ for viewers assigned to energy} \\ \text{treatment conditions,} \\ 0 \text{ otherwise;} \end{cases}$

Treatment$_2 = \begin{cases} 1 \text{ for viewers assigned to inflation} \\ \text{treatment conditions,} \\ 0 \text{ otherwise;} \end{cases}$

Treatment$_3 = \begin{cases} 1 \text{ for viewers assigned to defense} \\ \text{treatment conditions,} \\ 0 \text{ otherwise;} \end{cases}$

$$\text{Responsibility}_1 = \begin{cases} 1 \text{ for viewers assigned to high respon-} \\ \text{sibility energy conditions,} \\ 0 \text{ otherwise;} \end{cases}$$

$$\text{Responsibility}_2 = \begin{cases} 1 \text{ for viewers assigned to high respon-} \\ \text{sibility inflation conditions,} \\ 0 \text{ otherwise;} \end{cases}$$

$$\text{Responsibility}_3 = \begin{cases} 1 \text{ for viewers assigned to high respon-} \\ \text{sibility defense conditions,} \\ 0 \text{ otherwise;} \end{cases}$$

$$\text{Exposure}_1 = \begin{cases} 1.\text{for viewers assigned to high ex-} \\ \text{posure energy conditions,} \\ 0 \text{ otherwise;} \end{cases}$$

$$\text{Exposure}_2 = \begin{cases} 1 \text{ for viewers assigned to high ex-} \\ \text{posure inflation conditions,} \\ 0 \text{ otherwise;} \end{cases}$$

$$\text{Exposure}_3 = \begin{cases} 1 \text{ for viewers assigned to high ex-} \\ \text{posure defense conditions,} \\ 0 \text{ otherwise;} \end{cases}$$

The unprimed effects of problem performance ratings are assessed by β_1 (energy), β_2 (inflation), and β_3 (defense). The increase, if any, associated with exposure to minimal news coverage (low exposure, intermediate responsibility) is given by β_4 (energy), β_5 (inflation), and β_6 (defense). Whatever additional impact, if any, produced by high responsibility coverage is given by β_7 (energy), β_8 (inflation), and β_9 (defense). These estimated coefficients, which embody the hypothesis of interest here, also reflect controls on whatever additional impact is associated with exposure to many rather than few news stories (β'_{10}, β_{11}, and β_{12} for energy, inflation, and defense, respectively).

Experiment 12. The results displayed in table 9.2 are based on equations 9.3 and 9.4.

(9.3)   Overall performance $= \beta_0 + \beta_1$ (energy performance) $+$
β_2 (unemployment performance) $+$
β_3 (energy performance $\times$ treatment$_1$) $+$
β_4 (unemployment performance $\times$ treatment$_2$) $+$
β_5 (energy performance $\times$ treatment$_1$ $\times$ responsibility) $+$
β_6 (unemployment performance $\times$ treatment$_2$ $\times$ responsibility) $+ \varepsilon$

$$\text{where Treatment}_1 = \begin{cases} 1 \text{ for viewers assigned to energy} \\ \text{conditions,} \\ 0 \text{ otherwise;} \end{cases}$$

$$\text{Treatment}_2 = \begin{cases} 1 \text{ for viewers assigned to unemploy-} \\ \text{ment conditions,} \\ 0 \text{ otherwise;} \end{cases}$$

$$\text{Responsibility} = \begin{cases} -1 \text{ for viewers assigned to discount-} \\ \text{ing conditions,} \\ 0 \text{ for viewers assigned to agnostic} \\ \text{conditions,} \\ +1 \text{ for viewers assigned to augmenta-} \\ \text{tion conditions.} \end{cases}$$

As before, the unprimed effects of problem performance are given by β_1 (energy) and β_2 (unemployment). The basic priming effect is represented by β_3 (energy) and β_4 (unemployment). Finally, and of primary concern here, whatever additional impact is carried by the level of presidential responsibility conveyed by the news coverage is given by β_5 (energy) and β_6 (unemployment).

Experiment 13.

(9.4) Overall performance $= \beta_0 + \beta_1$(unemployment performance) $+$
β_2 (unemployment performance $\times$ treatment) $+$
β_3 (unemployment performance $\times$ treatment $\times$ responsibility)
$+ \varepsilon$

$$\text{Where Treatment} = \begin{cases} 1 \text{ for viewers assigned to the unem-} \\ \text{ployment conditions,} \\ 0 \text{ otherwise;} \end{cases}$$

$$\text{Responsibility} = \begin{cases} -1 \text{ for viewers assigned to unem-} \\ \text{ployment discounting condition,} \\ 0 \text{ for viewers assigned to unemploy-} \\ \text{ment agnostic condition,} \\ +1 \text{ for viewers assigned to unem-} \\ \text{ployment augmentation condition.} \end{cases}$$

As before, the unprimed effect of problem performance is given by β_1. The basic priming effect is tested by β_2. Whatever additional impact is due to level of presidential responsibility conveyed by the news coverage is given by β_3.

CHAPTER 10

The coefficients reported in table 10.1 were derived from the following equation:

(10.1)   General performance $= \beta_0 + \beta_1$ (problem performance) $+$
β_2 (audience factor) $+ \beta_3$ (treatment)
$+ \beta_4$ (problem performance $\times$ treatment)
$+ \beta_5$ (audience factor $\times$ problem performance)
$+ \beta_6$ (audience factor $\times$ problem performance $\times$ treatment)
$+ \varepsilon$

The coefficient β_1 tests the unprimed or baseline effects of problem performance; β_2 and β_3 capture the main effects of the audience factor and experimental treatment on general performance. The coefficient β_4 tests the basic priming effect. The coefficient β_5 tests for baseline audience differences in priming, i.e., differences in the effects of problem performance on general performance across different types of viewers among those shown no coverage of the target problem. Finally, of particular interest, β_6 gauges the extent to which the priming effect is strengthened or weakened among different types of viewers shown coverage of the target problem (over and above the naturally-occurring baseline effects picked up by β_5). It is β_6 that we report in table 10.1.

Since the interaction terms are highly colinear, it is impossible to estimate (with any reliability) an equation that includes the appropriate interaction terms for more than one audience characteristic at a time. Therefore we cannot isolate the *independent* effects of particular audience characteristics on the strength of the priming effect, holding constant the effects due to others.

To test whether *accessible* theories that implicate the president strengthen priming, we estimated equation 10.2.

(10.2)   General performance $= \beta_0 + \beta_1$ (problem performance) $+$
β_2 (recall) $+ \beta_3$ (theory) $+ \beta_4$ (treatment) $+$
β_5 (theory $\times$ problem performance) $+$
β_6 (theory $\times$ problem performance $\times$ treatment) $+$
β_7 (theory $\times$ problem performance $\times$ treatment $\times$ recall) $+ \varepsilon$

The coefficient of interest in equation 10.3 is β_7. A positively-signed and statistically significant β_7 means that priming is enhanced among viewers who hold theories that link the president to the problem, and who can recall information from relevant stories broadcast the week before (our crude measure of accessibility). It is β_7 that we report below:

Tacit Theory	Problem		
	Arms Control	Civil Rights	Unemployment
President is cause of problem	.15* (.12)	.27** (.15)	−.53 (.74)
President should solve problem	.13* (.11)	.29** (.19)	−.06 (.09)

Note: Number of participants = 63. Table entry is ordinary least squares regression co-efficient, with standard errors in parentheses.
*$p < .10$
**$p < .05$

CHAPTER 11

We tested for priming effects in experiment 10 by estimating the following equation:

(11.1)   DeNardis thermometer rating − Morrison thermometer rating = $\beta_0 + \beta_1$ (party identification) + β_2 (recognition) + β_3 (index of economic optimism) + β_4 ("likes" for DeNardis − "likes" for Morrison) + β_5 (index of economic optimism × economy treatment) + β_6 ("likes" for DeNardis − "likes" for Morrison × candidate treatment) + β_7 (party identification × control treatment) + β_8 (recognition × control treatment) + β_9 (control treatment) + β_{10} (candidate treatment) + ε

In this equation, β_1, β_2, β_3, and β_4 test the baseline effects of party identification, recognition, economic assessments, and candidate evaluations respectively. The coefficient β_5 captures the priming effect produced by news coverage of the economy. The larger this coefficient, the larger the increase in the effects of economic assessments on thermometer ratings. Similarly, the coefficient β_6 measures priming induced by news coverage of the candidates. Finally, β_7 and β_8 assess whether the effects of recognition and party affiliation were strengthened among viewers who saw no news coverage of the campaign.

We estimated equation 11.1 and found that the baseline effects of party and the two interaction terms associated with the control condition (β_7 and β_8) were indistinguishable from zero. We then eliminated these predictors and reestimated the equation. These are the results presented in table 11.1.

Experiment 7.

(11.2)   Overall performance $= \beta_0 + \beta_1$ (foreign affairs performance)
         $+ \beta_2$ (hostage crisis treatment)
         $+ \beta_3$ (Camp David treatment)
         $+ \beta_4$ (hostage crisis treatment $\times$ foreign affairs performance)
         $+ \beta_5$ (Camp David treatment $\times$ foreign affairs performance)
         $+ \varepsilon$

$$\text{Where Hostage Crisis Treatment} = \begin{cases} 1 \text{ if in hostage crisis} \\ \text{treatment,} \\ 0 \text{ otherwise;} \end{cases}$$

$$\text{Camp David Treatment} = \begin{cases} 1 \text{ if in Camp David} \\ \text{treatment,} \\ 0 \text{ otherwise.} \end{cases}$$

Equation 11.2 inlcudes the two main effects associated with being in the Hostage Crisis Treatment and with being in the Camp David Treatment because they approached statistical significance. The coefficients displayed in tables 11.2 and 11.3 thus reflect the full rank equation.

Notes

CHAPTER 1

1. This evidence is reviewed in Klapper (1960) and Kinder and Sears (1985).
2. Particularly in the able hands of Lippmann (1920, 1922, 1925); Lazarsfeld and Merton (1948); and Cohen (1963).
3. With a few important exceptions: Cohen (1963); Cook, Lomax, Tyler, Goetz, Gordon, Protess, Left, and Molotch (1983); Erbring, Miller and Goldenberg (1980); and MacKuen (1981, 1984).

CHAPTER 2

1. Each of the fourteen experiments is described in detail in Appendix A.
2. Of the fourteen experiments to be reported here, only two were conducted with college student populations: experiment 3 relied upon Yale University undergraduates; experiment 11 relied upon University of Michigan undergraduates. Both experiments were replicated by other experiments that drew upon community samples. Thus in no case do we reach conclusions or advance arguments based upon the responses of college students alone.

CHAPTER 3

1. In terms of the number of participants, experiment 1 was the smallest. As a general rule, our experimental conditions consisted of twenty participants or more. The exact numbers for all fourteen experiments are given in Appendix A.
2. The only exception to this pattern—the control group contained a significantly greater proportion of blacks (38 vs. 15 percent)—is innocuous, since participants' race proved to be unrelated to their beliefs about the importance of national defense.
3. The four items were worded as follows: "Shown below is a list of issues that have faced the nation in recent years. How important do you think each is?" The response options were "extremely important," "very important," "important," "not so important," and "not important at all." "How much do you care about each?" ("very much," "a lot," "some," "a little," "not at all"). "How much do you think people in government should worry about each?" ("a lot," "some," "a little," "not at all"). "How often do you talk

about these problems?" ("almost every day," "frequently," "sometimes," "rarely," "not at all"). In experiments 8 and 9 this fourth question was eliminated. In its place we asked participants "Compared with how you feel about other public issues, how strong are your feelings on these issues?" ("extremely strong," "very strong," "fairly strong," "not very strong").

4. The reliability of this composite index was gauged with Cronbach's Alpha, a measure of internal consistency. Across the four sequential experiments, the obtained coefficient ranged from .67 to .91, averaging .79. Coefficients of .65 or more are considered acceptable (see Bohrnstedt 1971).

5. Statistical significance refers to the certainty that the differences we detect are real—that they reflect real differences between conditions and not merely imprecision in the way we measure problem importance or "accidents" in the way we assign participants to treatment conditions. A statistically significant difference is one that we would expect to find over and over again, were we to follow the same procedure repeatedly. In the case of experiment 1, for example, participants assigned to the defense condition rated defense as more important after the experiment than before (an average difference of 20), while participants assigned to the control conditions rated defense just about the same afterwards as before (an average difference of 3). Can we be certain that the difference between the two conditions is real? We can. According to a 1-tailed t-test, the probability that the two groups do not differ is less than 5 in 100, written as $p < .05$. We will use this notation throughout, as a precise way of indicating the confidence that should be placed in our results. In general, we rely on directional (or 1-tailed) tests of significance. This means that we have strong expectations about the direction taken by whatever differences we find. And because statistical significance is more difficult to detect when the number of observations (or participants) is relatively small, as in our experiments, we tried to be comparatively generous in our interpretation of significance. (For further discussions of statistical significance, see Winkler and Hays 1975.)

6. Despite the striking evidence of agenda-setting in tables 3.1 and 3.2, the skeptical reader might still wonder whether our experiments were fortuitously (or even diabolically) timed to coincide with general increases in public concern for the problems we investigated. Perhaps the changes recorded in the tables were due not to experimentally-induced increases in television news coverage but to general forces operating outside the experiments. This is not the case. Not once did we detect comparable increases in importance judgments made by participants who were exposed to *no* coverage of the target problem. On technical grounds, we should probably have displayed these control group results in tables 3.1 and 3.2. This would have been technically appropriate but presentationally cumbersome. Because these results change absolutely nothing in our analysis, interpretations, or conclusions, we have chosen not to present them here.

7. All these experiments were designed with purposes in mind that went well beyond merely testing the basic agenda-setting hypothesis. For example, experiment 14 actually included two different versions of the drug smuggling condition. In one, the story on government efforts to reduce the flow of illegal drugs into the U.S. led off the newscast. In the other, the identical story appeared at about the midpoint. We will revisit experiment 14 in this more complex form in the next chapter. In the meantime, for the purpose of testing the agenda-setting hypothesis, it is appropriate to combine the two conditions, to treat experiment 14 as if it included only a single drug smuggling condition. The other assemblage experiments were similarly simplified.

8. Composite ratings in these assemblage experiments generally used the standard four questions described previously (see footnote 3). In experiment 13, however, only a single question was used. There participants were asked to rate the *seriousness* of each of several national problems.

9. The only anomaly in the various assemblage tests is located in experiment 13. As table 3.3 indicates, participants whose broadcasts included a story on energy subsequently declared energy costs to be a somewhat *less* serious problem than did those not shown the story, a difference that approached statistical significance. At the same time, they were *more likely* to nominate energy as an important national problem, as table 3.4 indicates. This pattern is puzzling, to say the least. Perhaps it can be explained in this way. The story on energy was unusual in that it dealt not with current conditions but with future developments—it warned that the energy crisis might soon reappear. It concentrated on the U.S.'s continued dependence on foreign sources of energy and on diminishing domestic supplies, with no explicit mention made of energy costs. Meanwhile, in the spring of 1983 as experiment 13 was being conducted, gasoline prices in Ann Arbor (as elsewhere) were drifting noticeably downwards. Perhaps, then, our experimental intervention did induce viewers to focus on energy, but with two quite different consequences. One was that viewers were more apt to say that energy in some general way constituted a serous national problem. The other was that viewers were prompted to mull over what they knew about energy from other sources, and because their own experiences told them that energy prices were declining, concluded that energy costs in particular could not be all that important.

10. Whether or not we were able to obtain reinterviews with our original participants was fortunately unrelated to their demographic characteristics, political values, and most significantly, to their judgments about national problems. This is reassuring that the reinterviewed groups are not peculiar; they look just like those who were not interviewed.

11. This analysis is reported in greater technical detail in Behr and Iyengar (1985).

12. Regular and equally-spaced observations are highly desirable, since they permit us to estimate the temporal dynamics of television coverage's in-

fluence on public opinion, e.g., how rapidly that influence appears and disappears.

13. We chose CBS over the other two major networks because between 1974 and 1980 CBS consistently attracted the largest audience. For our purposes, this choice is probably of little consequence. Studies of news coverage repeatedly show enormous overlap across the three networks (Iyengar 1979).

14. The control variables—the percent of responses devoted to inflation and to unemployment—have significant coefficients and are therefore retained in the equation so as to take into account the data transformation described in Appendix B. The coefficient for the percent of responses citing unemployment was $-.26$ with a standard error of $.13$. The coefficient for the percent citing inflation was $-.15$ with a standard error of $.10$.

15. For change in energy prices, $\beta = .13$, standard error $= .27$; for changes in heating oil prices, $\beta = -.04$, standard error $= .42$; for OPEC imports, $\beta = .00$, standard error $= .00$.

16. For percent change in CPI, $\beta = -.51$, standard error $= 1.76$; for percent change in CPI for food, $\beta = .06$, standard error $= 1.18$; for percent change in interest rates, $\beta = -.37$, standard error $= .62$.

17. Our results are generally consistent with MacKuen's (1981), based on different measures and a different estimating procedure.

CHAPTER 4

1. Cited in Nisbett and Ross (1980, 43).
2. Quotation appeared in *The Daily Oklahoma*, 16 March 1982.
3. Our manipulation of vividness can be summarized more precisely in terms of the amount of time devoted to interviews with victims. On average, vivid versions spent nearly one minute (fifty-two seconds) in this way while pallid versions ignored such interviews altogether. If we add to this the time devoted to close-up pictures of victims, then the averages are sixty-six seconds and nineteen seconds, respectively.
4. In statistical terms, this difference is described by the interaction between story (Chicago vs. CETA) and vividness (personal case vs. no personal case) in the unemployment treatments of experiment 6. The appropriate interaction terms approached statistical significance (for composite ratings, $F = 1.71$, $p < .19$; for spontaneous mentions, $F = 2.56$, $p < .11$).
5. We relied on a one hundred point "feeling thermometer" to measure participants' feelings toward blacks. Thermometer scores of zero indicate cold or unfavorable feelings, scores of one hundred indicate the opposite.
6. The stories were identical with one exception: the customary introduction associated with the lead story ("Good evening. This is the CBS Evening News," etc.) was deleted when the story was shifted to the middle of the broadcast.
7. We should point out that the judgments expressed by these eighty-three

participants in the questionnaire administered immediately after the broadcast resemble in the finest detail those provided by the entire sample. For the eighty-three, too, the lead versus middle position distinction mattered substantially in the importance attached to drug smuggling and rather little in the importance attached to public education.

8. This analysis is taken from Behr and Iyengar (1985). Details regarding the procedure and results can be found there. An abridged account of the estimation method is given in Appendix B.

CHAPTER 5

1. We find Erbring, Goldenberg, and Miller's (1980) argument more convincing than their evidence. We believe (as they seem to) that their research design does not provide a sensitive test of the readiness hypothesis. Our experiments represent an improvement in this respect: they get more directly at the interaction prediction that is at the heart of the readiness hypothesis.

2. The analysis of both experiments reported in detail in this chapter is confined to participants' spontaneous nomination of the nation's three most important problems. We do not report results based on participants' composite ratings of problem importance because, in trying to test the interaction hypothesis, we immediately encountered difficulties with both civil rights and social security. Blacks shown no stories about civil rights nevertheless rated civil rights as extremely important. The maximum composite rating is one hundred; blacks shown no stories about civil rights gave civil rights on average score of ninety-five. The elderly gave nearly as high ratings to saving the social security system: without benefit of any of our stories, elderly participants rated social security on average ninety. What this means is that blacks in the civil rights treatment and the elderly in the social security treatment cannot possibly be influenced by news coverage. They are already convinced that "their" problem is extremely significant. This makes it impossible to test the interaction hypothesis—that news coverage influences the personally affected more than those not personally affected. Fortunately, although blacks gave virtually maximum importance ratings to civil rights, as the elderly did to social security, neither spontaneously mentioned their problem with such frequency as to incapacitate tests of the interaction hypothesis. So our analysis reported here is confined to spontaneous mentions. We should add, however, that setting aside tests of the interaction hypothesis in the case of civil rights and social security, the results in both experiments based upon composite ratings conform in every detail to those reported here based upon spontaneous mentions.

3. The difference between blacks and whites on civil rights is statistically significant ($t = 2.90$, $p < .05$), as is the difference between the elderly and the young on social security ($t = 1.92$, $p < .05$). The difference between

the unemployed and the employed on the importance of unemployment as a national problem, however, is not ($t = .45$, $p > .50$).

4. All three interactions approach conventional levels of statistical significance: in the case of civil rights, $F_{2,104} = 2.40$, $p < .10$; for unemployment, $F_{2,104} = 2.57$, $p < .10$; for social security, $F_{2,104} = 2.16$, $p < .10$.

5. Students, housewives, part-time workers and the retired were excluded from this experiment.

6. Because we had no control over the newscasts that participants in the control group watched during the week preceding the posttest, a fair question is whether they really constitute an appropriate control group. It seems safe to say that they do. In the first place, had they watched the national news religiously (and had they somehow been able to watch all three network newscasts every day), they would have seen just three stories on unemployment. In the second place, after the experiment was completed, we asked these participants to identify as many stories as they could from the news programs they had seen during the past week. A total of six participants mentioned one employment-related story. The remainder (twenty-six) mentioned none at all. This provides some reassurance that participants in the control group were, in fact, exposed to less coverage of unemployment than participants in the experimental condition.

7. $t = .98$, $p < .17$.

8. $t = 2.30$, $p < .01$.

9. $F_{1,66} = 2.07$, $p < .16$. This same pattern was evident in pretest to posttest changes among employed and unemployed participants shown news coverage of unemployment. That is, references to unemployment increased significantly among both groups, but the increase was more prominent among the employed. For the unemployed group, the percentages naming unemployment as one of the country's most serious problems went from 56 percent to 81 percent ($t = 2.24$, $p < .02$); for the employed, the corresponding percentage actually doubled, going from 45 percent to 90 percent ($t = 3.34$, $p < .01$).

10. Alternatively, the apparent power of race and age in our results could reflect some flaw in our procedures, despite our best efforts—the inevitably artificial nature of experimental settings, or peculiar biases in the selection of participants. To test this alternative possibility and thereby gain a better sense of the generality of the experimental results, we turned once again to evidence provided by national surveys. In this instance, we relied upon a pair of surveys carried out by the Center for Political Studies. As part of the Center's continuing investigation of U.S. national elections, a representative cross-section of Americans of voting age ($N = 1614$) was questioned in person during September and October of 1980, at the climax of the Carter-Reagan presidential campaign. Another cross-section ($N = 1418$) was interviewed in the fall of 1982, immediately following the midterm congressional elections. Thus the 1980 survey preceded our experiments; the 1982 survey followed them. In both surveys, interviewers

asked Americans to name "the most important problems the government in Washington should try to take care of," and then recorded as many as three answers. Because the two surveys also contained an extensive battery of demographic questions including race, employment status, and age,·they enabled us to test the impact of personal predicaments on views of national problems, free from whatever distortion may have been introduced by our experimental settings or by our less than fully representative samples.

We combined the two surveys and then computed the degree of association between personal predicaments and national views for each of the three problems examined in our experiments: civil rights, unemployment, and social security. These results indicated, just as our experiments did, strong effects of race on the importance of civil rights, strong effects of age on the importance of social security, and somewhat more modest effects of employment status on the importance of unemployment. On average, blacks were nearly five times more likely to name some aspect of civil rights as one of the country's most important problems than were whites (2.3 percent vs. 0.5 percent; Chi-square = 13.90, $p < .01$). The elderly were more than twice as likely to nominate maintaining the social security system as one of the country's most important problems than were the young (17.3 percent vs. 7.9 percent; Chi-square = 27.07, $p < .01$). And Americans out of work were somewhat more likely to name unemployment as one of the nation's most important problems than were the employed (56.4 percent vs. 39.5 percent; Chi-square = 19.07, $p < .07$).

All these results stand up to a more rigorous analysis in which the effects of race, age, and employment status are considered simultaneously. In this analysis, the likelihood of mentioning civil rights as a serious national problem is powerfully predicted by race; the likelihood of mentioning social security is powerfully predicted by age; and the likelihood of mentioning unemployment is predicted (though not as powerfully as in the other two instances) by employment status. These results, based on a series of multivariate probit analyses, are shown in Appendix B.

In short, the survey results offer reassurance about our experimental findings. It now seems clear that the substantial direct effects of personal predicaments found in our experiments reflect not some peculiarity in our procedures but rather some special features of civil rights and social security.

11. Downs (1972, 38) argues that problems are often of this character: "American public attention rarely remains sharply focused upon any one domestic issue for very long—even if it involves a continuing problem of crucial importance to society. Instead, a systematic 'issue-attention cycle' seems strongly to influence public attitudes and behavior concerning most key domestic problems. Each of these problems suddenly leaps into prominence, remains there for a short period, and then—though still largely unresolved—gradually fades from the center of public attention."

CHAPTER 6

1. We asked participants for "the highest grade of school" they had completed and then classified them into two categories: "high school or less" and "some college or more."

2. This was the question: "Generally speaking, do you consider yourself a Democrat, a Republican, an Independent, or something else?"

3. The questions were worded as follows: (1) "Some people follow what's going on in government and public affairs most of the time, whether there's an election going on or not. Others aren't that interested. Would you say that you follow what's going on in government most of the time, some of the time, only now and then, or hardly at all?"; (2) "When you read the paper, how much attention do you pay to news about government and politics?" The response options were "a great deal of attention," "some attention," and "don't pay much attention."

4. Participants were asked "Do you read a newspaper regularly?" and "How often do you watch the *national* news on television in the evening?"

5. The question was "How often do you discuss government and politics with people you know?" The response options were "frequently," "now and then," "rarely," and "never."

6. More precisely, this is an index of *electoral* activism. Participants were asked whether they had voted in the last presidential election, attended a political meeting or rally, contributed money to a candidate, placed a bumper sticker on their car, or persuaded someone to vote for a particular candidate.

7. Participants answered three or four questions concerning each problem. The questions were designed to assess awareness and recognition of events, policies, public officials, or governmental institutions. The answers were coded as correct or incorrect and then summed to form an index. Each index, associated with each problem, was then standardized and finally pooled together. The questions are listed below.

Inflation
1. Based on the most recent statistics, what is the projected annual rate of inflation?
2. What would the "Kemp-Roth Bill" do, if passed by Congress?
3. What is "supply-side economics" about?

Pollution
1. Who is the current Secretary of the Interior?
2. Which federal agency has the primary responsibility for controlling contamination of the nation's air, water and soil?
3. Can you name any private organization that works to protect the environment?

Unemployment
1. Can you name the head of a major labor union?
2. What is the current national unemployment rate?

3. Which cabinet-level, federal department has the primary responsibility for the employment situation in the country?
4. Among which group of Americans is unemployment the highest?

Defense
1. What is the name of the military alliance made up of the Soviet Union and several East European nations?
2. The Reagan administration has proposed significant increases in defense spending. Can you identify any of the new weapon systems being considered by the administration?
3. Who is the Secretary of Defense?

Civil Rights
1. What important piece of civil rights legislation, first enacted in 1965, was recently extended by the Congress?
2. Can you identify the only black judge on the U.S. Supreme Court?
3. Very briefly, what did the "Bakke Case" involve?
4. Can you name the black member of the Reagan Cabinet?

Arms Control
1. What is the name of the military alliance made up of the Soviet Union and several East European nations?
2. The Reagan administration has proposed significant increases in defense spending. Can you identify any of the new weapon systems being considered by the administration?
3. Can you identify a specific area of disagreement between the Soviet Union and the U.S. in the arms control talks between the two nations?
4. What is a tactical nuclear weapon?
5. Who is Secretary of Defense?

8. Combining the three experiments is highly desirable for the purpose of subgroup analysis. Separating participants into classes according to their education, party identification, and political involvement requires a sufficient number of participants to enable analysis to reach reliable conclusions. If we were to examine our experiments separately, we would have too few participants in each subgroup. Therefore we have pooled the experiments together. However, pooling does require a strong assumption: that whatever interactions are actually to be found between network coverage on the one hand and viewers' education, party identification, and involvement on the other, are comparable across different national problems. If the poorly-educated are influenced more than the well-educated by network coverage of inflation, they must also be more influenced by coverage of environmental problems for our analysis to be taken seriously. We think this is a reasonable assumption to make for the characteristics under investigation here. Moreover, as we will see, the results we obtain from the pooled analysis are consistent and intelligible.
9. The average correlation between education and the various aspects of in-

volvement is .16; between party identification and the aspects of involvement, it is .14.

10. On the basic distinction, see McGuire (1968); for useful political applications, see Sears and Whitney (1973), MacKuen (1984), and Zaller (1986).

Chapter 7

1. Throughout the present chapter and for most of those that follow, our analysis concentrates on evaluations of the *president*. Nevertheless, we mean priming to apply to political evaluation in general. Chapter 11 provides evidence on voters' evaluations of U.S. House candidates that is reassuring on this score.

2. Additional experimental work in the same spirit is summarized by Higgins and King 1981; Schuman and Presser 1981; and Fiske and Taylor 1984.

3. Although our argument concentrates on the consequences of accessibility for *evaluation*, it is clear that accessibility also has implications for how new information is *interpreted* (see, for example, Higgins, Rholes, and Jones 1977; Srull and Wyer 1979).

4. The vigilant reader, should there still be one, may remember that experiment 2 included *three* conditions: the two we just mentioned plus another in which newscasts emphasized problems of pollution. Unfortunately, by the (bad) luck of the draw, the pollution condition ended up with significantly fewer Democrats than did the other two conditions ($p < .03$). This poses no serious difficulty for testing agenda-setting—since party identification is essentially uncorrelated with problem priorities—so we reported the results from all three conditions of experiment 2 in chapter 3. The uneven distribution of party identification does pose difficulties for our tests of priming, however, since evaluations of the president are so heavily colored by partisanship. For the purpose of testing priming, therefore, we put the pollution condition aside.

5. In all instances in experiments 1, 2, and 9, participants answered these performance questions by selecting among five options, ranging from "very good" to "very poor." Unless otherwise noted, all our tests of priming are based on questions that follow this format exactly.

6. Here and throughout the analysis of priming, we report *unstandardized* regression coefficients. We do so because our intent is to compare the impact of problem performance ratings on overall assessments across groups of participants assigned to different experimental conditions (and later on, across equations associated with different dependent variables). Basing such comparisons on standardized coefficients would be misleading should the variances of these measures differ across groups or equations (see Duncan 1975).

7. For example, participants in the civil rights condition watched a news story that detailed President Reagan's opposition to extending the 1965 Voting Rights Act. The unemployment treatment featured stories describing the massive cuts in job training programs implemented by the Reagan

administration. Finally, viewers in the arms control treatment were given stories detailing the ominous increases in tension between the U.S. and USSR.

8. How can we be certain that these priming effects are due to differences in television news coverage and not to preexisting differences between participants assigned to different treatment conditions? Perhaps those who watched newscasts laced with stories about civil rights were preoccupied with civil rights to begin with? This is possible, but assigning participants to conditions on a random basis makes this interpretation implausible. We can provide further assurance on this point, however, by taking advantage of the fact that participants in experiment 8 were asked to evaluate President Reagan's performance both before the experiment began and afterward. If random assignment was successful, then we should find estimated priming effects based on *pre*experimental ratings to be essentially zero, since priming had not yet begun. In fact, the effects *are* essentially zero: the relevant coefficients are .17 for arms control performance ratings, .05 for civil rights, and −.17 for unemployment. All are statistically indistinguishable from zero.

9. Experiments 3 and 4 also permit testing whether priming is greater after exposure to *many* stories about a target problem rather than after only *a few*. In neither experiment did we find any evidence to support this hypothesis.

10. The contrast between sequential and assemblage results cannot be explained by differences in the problems that served as the centers of attention in the two types of experiments. Inflation and defense served as target problems in both sequential and assemblage experiments, and in each instance, the same contrast emerged. So, for example, we found a substantial priming effect with inflation performance ratings in experiment 2 (a sequential test) and a modest priming effect with inflation performance ratings in experiment 4 (an assemblage test).

CHAPTER 8

1. Respondents were asked: "I am going to read a list of words and phrases people use to describe political figures. For each, please tell me whether the word or phrase describes the candidate I name extremely well, quite well, not too well, or not well at all. Think about Jimmy Carter. The first word on our list is 'moral.' In your opinion does the word 'moral' describe Carter extremely well, quite well, not too well, or not well at all?" And so on through a list of seven traits in all: dishonest, weak, knowledgeable, power-hungry, inspiring, and provides strong leadership. The list was then repeated for Ronald Reagan.

2. We do not mean to make too fine a point here. It is easy enough to demonstrate the intrusion of logically irrelevant factors in everyday judgments (Nisbett and Wilson 1977).

3. Like ratings of the president's success on specific problems and evaluations of his general performance, the competence and integrity indexes range in principle from one to five.

4. Performance questions regarding inflation, energy, unemployment, and the hostage crisis followed the identical format. Respondents were first asked: "Do you approve or disapprove of Jimmy Carter's handling of inflation (the energy problem/unemployment/or the crisis brought about by the taking of Americans as hostages in Iran)?" Those who indicated that they approved or disapproved were then asked: "Do you approve (disapprove) strongly or not strongly?" Regarding the Soviet invasion, respondents were first told: "As you may know, in late December Soviet troops moved into Afghanistan. So far the President has protested this Soviet action by cutting back on American trade, diplomatic and cultural ties with the Soviet Union." They were then asked: "Considering the U.S. response thus far, would you say that Jimmy Carter has reacted too strongly to the Soviet Union, not strongly enough, or has the response been about right?"

5. With respect to overall performance, respondents were first asked, "Do you approve or disapprove of the way Jimmy Carter is handling his job as President?" and then, "Do you approve (disapprove) strongly or not strongly?" With respect to character, see note 1. Weak (reflected), knowledgeable, inspiring, and provides strong leadership represent competence; moral, dishonest (reflected), and power-hungry (reflected) represent integrity.

6. With respect to problem performance ratings, respondents were asked: "Do you approve or disapprove of Ronald Reagan's handling of arms control (unemployment/national defense/inflation)?" General assessments were solicited exactly as in the 1980 National Election Studies, with Ronald Reagan replacing Jimmy Carter (see note 5 above).

7. This does not mean that citizens gave the two presidents equal marks. Far from it. In the fall of 1982, a (bare) majority approved of President Reagan's performance on inflation (50.1 percent). Two years before, in the fall of 1980, less than one-quarter of the public approved President Carter's performance on inflation (23.5 percent). Inflation was consequential for both presidents, but it helped Reagan while it hurt Carter.

8. The survey tests of the gradient hypothesis are not fully comparable to the experimental results. In the experimental case, we reported the impact of problem performance ratings on general assessments that was due to the problem being primed. This impact is over and above the "baseline" relationship between performance ratings and general assessments. In the survey case, we have no convincing way to distinguish between those respondents who were primed with news about a particular problem from those who were not. Consequently, the survey results combine the two effects: the findings reported in tables 8.2 and 8.3 reflect both the baseline (long-term) effects of problem ratings on general assessments and whatever effects have resulted from recent media priming. Fortunately, this difference is not a serious one for the purpose of testing the gradient hy-

pothesis. If we return to the six experiments and report, not the effect due to priming, but the effect due to priming *plus* the baseline effect, the same pattern emerges: the effect is greater for overall performance than for either competence or integrity; the effect is generally greater for competence than for integrity in the case of Carter; and the effect is generally greater for integrity than for competence in the case of Reagan. This essential similarity strengthens the case for treating the experimental and survey results as complementary.

CHAPTER 9

1. For a general psychological analysis of this concept of responsibility, see Fincham and Jaspars (1982).
2. All participants in the control condition were questioned approximately four weeks after treatment participants. There were no statistically significant differences in demographic characteristics and basic political attitudes (party identification, liberal-conservative orientation) between these control group students and students in the four treatment conditions.
3. Typical of a high responsibility story was a report on President Carter's veto of a defense appropriations bill that would have added two aircraft carriers to the navy's fleet. The report included comments by several congressmen critical of Carter and his defense policy while Carter, in turn, attacked Congress for proposing unnecessary military expenditures. By contrast, stories that made up the bulk of the intermediate responsibility conditions made no reference to the president or his policies. In one such story, for example, North Atlantic Treaty Organization (NATO) defense ministers were shown gathering to discuss common strategy in the event of Soviet aggression in Europe.
4. In the case of energy, participants in the augmentation condition saw a story that traced the growing dependence of the U.S. on foreign energy sources to inaction by the Reagan administration. In the discounting condition, participants watched a story that featured experts warning of a future energy crisis because of war in the Middle East and Americans' continued love affair with the automobile, particularly with large gasoline-guzzling automobiles. Finally, in the agnostic condition, participants saw a story describing how, in various ingenious ways, Americans were saving energy.

CHAPTER 10

1. We relied on just three sequential experiments and ignored the fourth (experiment 9), for two reasons. First, one-half of the participants in experiment 9 were by design unemployed. This feature is indispensable to the purpose of that experiment, but creates trouble for the purpose of investigating characteristics of viewers that might make them *generally* susceptible or *generally* immune to priming, which is our purpose here. Second,

of all our tests of priming, experiment 9 furnished the weakest support—a small and statistically unreliable priming effect (table 7.1). This provides no basis for an inquiry into individual differences in susceptibility to priming. On these two grounds, we set experiment 9 aside.

2. Participants were first asked whether, in their estimation, the problem of unemployment (arms control/civil rights [depending on condition]) had worsened, improved, or remained unchanged during the past year. Then they were asked "Why do you say so? (just give the most important reason)."

3. Participants were asked "Who do you think is most responsible for doing something about unemployment (arms control/civil rights [again, depending on condition])?"

4. On a few problems, Independents were somewhat more susceptible to priming than were partisans (arms control and pollution); on others, they were somewhat less (unemployment and inflation); on the remainder, they were neither more nor less susceptible to priming.

5. These results, based on sequential tests, are inconsistent with results we reported in an earlier publication, based on a single assemblage experiment (Iyengar, Kinder, Peters, and Krosnick 1984). In the earlier report, we found that priming was diminished among problem "experts"; here we find that expertise in particular and involvement in general seem quite irrelevant to priming. We suspect that the inconsistency can be traced to differences in the designs. In assemblage experiments, experts show less priming than do novices because their standards are more securely anchored. In sequential experiments, experts tend to show less priming than do novices for the same reason, but they tend to show more priming because they are likely to be paying more attention, and more efficient attention, to the news stories. The result is that priming is inversely related to expertise in assemblage experiments and unrelated to expertise in sequential experiments. Since sequential experiments more closely resemble viewers' actual encounters with television news, we place more faith in these results than those based on assemblage experiments.

6. The postexperiment questionnaire requested participants to list any "thoughts, feelings, and reactions" they might have experienced in response to three of the stories we had inserted into their broadcasts. The stories were identified by means of a brief label. Depending on the degree of detail they provided, we classified participants into either high or low recall categories.

7. Consistent with this claim is our evidence that the politically involved are naturally more inclined to judge a president according to his performance on national problems than are uninvolved viewers. This evidence comes from control group participants in experiments 1, 2, and 8—those who were exposed to no news about the target problem. Among such participants, the politically involved were generally more likely to judge the president according to his performance on the target problem than were

the uninvolved. Eighteen out of forty-eight separate tests were statistically significant. Of these, fifteen indicated that the involved were more likely to evaluate the president in performance terms than were the uninvolved.

CHAPTER 11

1. This experiment was conceived and conducted by Roy Behr, as part of his Ph.D. dissertation research in the department of Political Science at Yale University.
2. Corrected Chi-square = 5.33 with 1 degree of freedom, $p = .021$.
3. For DeNardis, 1.42 replies on average versus 1.06: $p = .37$ by F-test. For Morrison, 1.32 replies on average versus .89: $p = .17$.
4. For DeNardis, Chi-square with 5 degrees of freedom = 3.96, $p = .56$; for Morrison, Chi-square with 5 degrees of freedom = 4.94, $p = .42$. Participants assigned to candidate coverage were also more likely to agree or disagree *strongly* with the candidates. For DeNardis, $p = .17$ by F-test; for Morrison, $p = .08$.
5. For DeNardis, $p = .68$ by F-test; for Morrison, $p = .53$.
6. These results are corroborated by Goldenberg and Traugott's survey-based analysis of incumbents and challengers running for Congress in 1978 (Goldenberg and Traugott 1984).
7. On average, participants in the control treatment expressed opinions on the economy 98 percent of the time while participants in the economy treatment did so 96 percent of the time.
8. Following the election we attempted to contact as many participants as possible to ascertain how they had voted. We were able to obtain this information from twenty-eight of the original fifty-six. Of these, twenty-six voted consistently with their thermometer ratings.
9. Participants were asked if they generally thought of themselves as Democrats, Republicans, Independents, or something else.
10. Participants were asked to name the two candidates. Those who correctly identified DeNardis but were unable to name Morrison received a score of +1; those unable to name either candidate or who named both candidates got scores of 0; and those who named Morrison but not DeNardis received scores of −1. Thus the higher the score, the greater the relative visibility of the incumbent.
11. Participants were asked "Is there anything in particular you like about Larry DeNardis? What?" They were permitted to list up to three characteristics. The identical question was asked with respect to Morrison. We subtracted the number of positive qualities ascribed to Morrison from the number ascribed to DeNardis. This measure thus ranges from −3 (three likes mentioned for Morrison, none for DeNardis) to + 3 (three likes mentioned for DeNardis, none for Morrison).
12. We constructed an index of economic pessimism based on answers to four

separate questions. First, participants indicated whether they thought the economy had improved, stayed the same, or worsened over the past year. They also indicated whether the economy would improve, stay the same, or deteriorate during the coming year. Participants then evaluated President Reagan's performance in "handling the economy" on a scale from "very poor job" to "very good job." Finally, participants indicated whether problems of the economy would be handled better by the Republicans or the Democrats. Responses to these questions were then added together (the index ranges from four to fourteen). Low scores indicate pessimism about the economy, negative evaluations of Reagan's economic record, and the perception that Democrats deal with economic problems more effectively than Republicans do. Conversely, high scores indicate upbeat perceptions of the economy, favorable evaluations of Reagan's economic performance, and the perception that Republicans are better than Democrats in solving economic problems.

13. This effect is represented in statistical terms by the interaction between party identification and assignment to the economy treatment. In an equation predicting assessments of economic conditions, this interaction approaches statistical significance: $\beta = 1.68$, $se = 1.69$, $t = 0.99$, $p < .18$.

14. In statistical terms, this effect is represented by the interaction between party identification and assignment to the candidate treatment. In an equation predicting the difference between positive qualities mentioned about DeNardis and positive qualities mentioned about Morrison, this interaction is marginally significant: $\beta = 1.09$, $se = .87$, $t = 1.27$, $p < .10$.

15. These figures are taken from *The Almanac of American Politics, 1984*. Vote percentage reflects division of the two-party totals.

16. This is the point of view taken by Patrick Caddell, pollster to President Carter. The sharp shift to Reagan in the last days of the campaign was produced, Caddell thought, by "a change in the weights that people were giving the various aspects of the campaign. . . . Iranian developments that final weekend changed the mindset of voters as they prepared to cast their ballots" (*Public Opinion* 1981, 63).

17. The exact questions were:
    (1) How well do you feel President Carter handled the Iranian hostage crisis generally?
    (very well / good / fair / poor / don't know)
    (2) How well do you feel President Carter handled the Camp David peace treaty between Egypt and Israel?
    (very well / good / fair / poor / don't know)
    (3) Some people say that respect for America by people in foreign countries has declined. Others think America is respected as much now as before. How much do you think people in foreign countries respect Americans these days?
    (much more than they used to / somewhat more than they used to / somewhat less than they used to / much less than they used to / don't know)

and

How would you grade former President Carter's performance in the following area:

Keeping America respected around the world?

(very good / good / fair / poor / very poor / don't know)

(4) How would you grade former President Carter's performance in the following areas:

dealing with foreign countries?

and

peacefully solving world problems?

(very good / good / fair / poor / very poor / don't know)

18. This claim presumes that voters decide whether or not to support a president running for reelection at least partly on the basis of how they evaluate his past performance in office. This is true as a general matter (Fiorina 1981) and was certainly true for the 1980 National Election Study. For example, we found that Democrats who approved of Carter's performance were nearly unanimous in their intention to vote for Carter (96 percent), whereas Democrats who disapproved of Carter's performance intended to defect in huge numbers (only 36 percent declared their intention to vote for Carter).

CHAPTER 12

1. This is not always the case. When a problem has received persistent coverage, eventually a point is reached at which the victims of the problem have reached maximal levels in the importance they attach to the problem. At this point, those not personally affected by the problem are affected more by news coverage. Experiment 9 presents a case of this reversal with respect to unemployment, conducted as it was in the depths of a deep recession.

2. And in work recently completed by others; most notably, Erbring, Goldenberg, and Miller 1980; MacKuen 1981, 1983, 1984.

3. For a careful analysis of district-to-district variation in media coverage of congressional elections, see Behr 1985.

4. The literature on political persuasion is huge. For reviews, see Sears and Whitney (1973); Klapper (1960); Kinder and Sears (1985).

5. Braestrup's indictment was directed at the prestige media in general. In Braestrup's view, Tet was misinterpreted by ABC, NBC, and CBS, but also by *The Washington Post, The New York Times,* the UPI and AP wire services, and by *Time* and *Newsweek* alike.

6. For evidence on shifts in public opinion after Tet, see Schuman (1973).

7. Certainly Chomsky (1978) does not. More generally, reviews of Braestrup's work have depended sharply on the reviewer's own political views (Wise 1979).

8. Rubin's conclusion is based on a comparison between the CBS Evening News and several major newspapers from 1963 to 1975.

9. For a view that emphasizes more the president's ability to set the public agenda, see MacKuen (1983).

10. The evidence on this point is extensive. See, for example, Hibbs, Rivers, and Vasilatos (1982a, 1982b); Kernell (1978); MacKuen (1983); and Ostrom and Simon (1985).

11. ABC News Poll, Survey #0041.

12. One implication of this analysis is that viewers should differ from one another in their vulnerability to television news, depending on the credibility they attribute to the networks. Viewers who regard the networks as paragons of virtue should be especially influenced by television news while those who look at the networks with suspicion should be influenced least. Indeed, this appears to be so. In several of our experiments, participants were asked to rate the objectivity and accuracy of the national newscasts. As expected, viewers who regarded the networks as authoritative sources were influenced more by the news stories than were those who regarded ABC, CBS, and NBC less highly. These results are reported in Iyengar and Kinder (1986a).

13. For evidence on this point, see Patterson and McClure (1976); Patterson (1980); Graber (1980); and Robinson and Sheehan (1983).

14. Other critics go further, suggesting that television has spawned a new breed of telegenic candidates who lack traditional ties to parties or interest groups (see for example Polsby 1983; Postman 1985).

15. Robinson's experimental results in fact closely resemble those reported by Hovland, Lumsdaine, and Sheffield (1949), based on an extensive and well-controlled series of experiments conducted during World War II. Hovland's team found that although propaganda films developed by the U.S. War Department were highly effective in passing information along, they were highly ineffective in changing attitudes. This result contributed heavily to Klapper's (1960) influential conclusion of minimal effects.

16. This evidence appears in Graber (1980), Hofstetter (1976), and Robinson and Sheehan (1983).

17. Our conception of objectivity relies heavily on Hallin (1986); also helpful were Cohen (1963), Sigal (1973), and Tuchman (1972). On the development of objectivity as a professional ideology, see Schudson (1978).

18. This point is argued in somewhat different ways by Arlen (1976, "Spokespeople"), Sigal (1973), Epstein (1973), Gans (1979), Schudson (1978), and Hallin (1986).

Bibliography

Abelson, R. P. 1959. Modes of resolution of belief dilemmas. *Journal of Conflict Resolution* 3:343–52.

Arlen, M. J. 1976. *The view from highway 1*. New York: Farrar, Straus & Giroux.

Arterton, F. C. 1984. *Media politics: The news strategies of presidential campaigns*. Lexington, Mass.: D. C. Heath.

Asch, S. E. 1946. Forming impressions of personality. *Journal of Abnormal and Social Psychology* 41:258–90.

Barber, J. D. 1980. *The pulse of politics*. New York: W. W. Norton.

Barone, M., and G. Ujifusa, eds. 1984. *The almanac of American politics*. Washington, D.C.: National Journal Inc.

Bartels, L. M. 1985. Expectations and preferences in presidential nominating campaigns. *American Political Science Review* 79:804–15.

Behr, R. L. 1985. The effects of media on voters' considerations in presidential and congressional elections. Ph.D. diss., Department of Political Science, Yale Univ.

Behr, R. L., and S. Iyengar. 1985. Television news, real-world cues, and changes in the public agenda. *Public Opinion Quarterly* 49:38–57.

Bishop, G. F., R. W. Oldendick, and A. J. Tuchfarber. 1982. Political information processing: Question order and context effects. *Political Behavior* 4:177–200.

Bohrnstedt, G. 1971. Reliability and validity assessment in attitude measurement. In *Attitude measurement*, ed. by G. Summers. Chicago: Rand McNally.

Bower, R. T. 1985. *The changing television audience in America*. New York: Columbia Univ. Press.

Braestrup, P. 1977/83. *Big story*. New Haven: Yale Univ. Press.

Brody, R. A., and B. I. Page. 1973. Indifference, alienation, and rational decisions. *Public Choice* 15:1–17.

———. 1975. The impact of events on presidential popularity: The Johnson and Nixon administrations. In *Perspectives on the presidency*, ed. by A. Wildavsky. Boston: Little, Brown & Co.

Bunce, V. 1981. *Do new leaders make a difference?* Princeton: Princeton Univ. Press.

Burstein, P. 1979. Public opinion, demonstrations, and the passage of anti-discrimination legislation. *Public Opinion Quarterly* 43:157–72.

Burstein, P., and W. Freudenburg. 1978. Changing public policy: The impact of public opinion, antiwar demonstrations, and war costs on Senate voting on Vietnam War Motions. *American Journal of Sociology* 84:99–122.

Cameron, D. R. 1977. The expansion of the public economy. *American Political Science Review* 72:1243–61.

Campbell, D. T. 1969a. Prospective: Artifact and control. In *Artifact in behavioral research*, ed. by R. Rosenthal and R. Rosnow. New York: Academic Press.

———— 1969b. Reforms as experiments. *American Psychologist* 24:409–29.

Cartwright, D., and A. Zander. 1968. *Group dynamics: Research and theory.* 3d ed. New York: Harper & Row.

Chomsky, N. 1978. The U.S. media and the Tet offensive. *Race and Class* 20:21–39.

Clarke, P., and S. H. Evans. 1983. *Covering campaigns: Journalism in Congressional elections.* Stanford: Stanford Univ. Press.

Cohen, B. 1963. *The press and foreign policy.* Princeton: Princeton Univ. Press.

Converse, P. E. 1964. Belief systems in mass publics. In *Ideology and discontent,* ed. by D. E. Apter. New York: Free Press.

———— 1972. Change in the American electorate. In *The human meaning of social change,* ed. by A. Campbell and P. E. Converse. New York: Russell Sage Foundation.

Cook, F. Lomax, T. R. Tyler, E. G. Goetz, M. T. Gordon, D. Protess, D. R. Leff, and H. L. Molotch. 1983. Media and agenda-setting: Effects on the public, interest group leaders, policy makers, and policy. *Public Opinion Quarterly* 47:16–35.

Cover, A. D., and D. R. Mayhew. 1977. Congressional dynamics and the decline of competitive Congressional elections. In *Congress reconsidered,* ed. by L. C. Dodd and B. I. Oppenheimer. New York: Praeger.

Dahl, R. A., and C. E Lindblom. 1953. *Politics, economics, and welfare.* New York: Harper & Row.

Downs, A. 1972. Up and down with ecology—the "issue attention cycle." *Public Interest* 28:38–50.

Duncan, O. D. 1975. *An introduction to structural equation models.* New York: Academic Press.

Edelman, M. 1964. *The symbolic uses of politics.* Urbana: Univ. of Illinois Press.

Eldersveld, S. 1956. Experimental propaganda techniques and voting behavior. *American Political Science Review* 50:154–65.

Epstein, E. 1973. *News from nowhere.* New York: Random House.

Erbring, L., E. Goldenberg, and A. Miller. 1980. Front-page news and real-world cues: A new look at agenda-setting. *American Journal of Political Science* 24:16–49.

FCC. Editorializing by broadcast licensees. Document no. 856, 1 June 1949.

Fair, R. 1970. The estimation of simultaneous equation models with lagged endogenous variables and first order serial autocorrelated errors. *Econometrica* 38:507–16.

Fincham, F. D., and J. M. Jaspars. 1980. Attributions of responsibility: From man the scientist to man as lawyer. *Advances in Experimental Social Psychology* 13:82–139.

Fiorina, M. P. 1981. *Retrospective voting in American national elections.* New Haven: Yale Univ. Press.

Fiorina, M. P., and C. Plott. 1978. Committee decisions under majority rule: An experimental study. *American Political Science Review* 72:575–98.

Fischhoff, B., P. Slovic, and S. Lichtenstein. 1980. Knowing what you want: Measuring labile values. In *Cognitive processes in choice and decision behavior,* ed. by T. Wallsten. Hillsdale, N.J.: Erlbaum.

Fiske, S. T., and D. R. Kinder. 1981. Involvement, expertise and schema use: Evidence from political cognition. In *Cognition, social interaction and personality,* ed. by N. Cantor and J. Kihlstrom. Hillsdale: N.J.: Erlbaum.

Fiske, S. T., and S. E. Taylor. 1984. *Social cognition.* Reading, Mass.: Addison-Wesley.

Funkhouser, G. R. 1973. The issues of the sixties: An exploratory study in the dynamics of public opinion. *Public Opinion Quarterly* 37:62–75.

Gans, H. 1979. *Deciding what's news.* New York: Vintage Books.

Gitlin, T. 1980. *The whole world is watching: Mass media in the making and unmaking of the new left.* Berkeley: Univ. of California Press.

Goldenberg, E. N., and M. W. Traugott. 1984. *Campaigning for Congress.* Washington, D.C.: Congressional Quarterly Press.

Gosnell, H. F. 1927. *Machine politics: Chicago model.* Chicago: Univ. of Chicago Press.

Graber, D. A. 1980. *Mass media and American politics.* Washington, D.C.: Congressional Quarterly Press.

Greenstein, F. I. 1978. Change and continuity in the modern presidency. In *The new American political system,* ed. by A. King. Washington, D.C.: American Enterprise Institute.

Grossman, M. B., and M. J. Kumar. 1981. *Portraying the president.* Baltimore: Johns Hopkins Univ. Press.

Hallin, D. C. 1984. The media, the war in Vietnam, and political support: A critique of the thesis of an oppositional media. *Journal of Politics* 46:2–24.

——— 1985. The American news media: A critical theory perspective. In *Critical theory and public policy,* ed. by J. Forester. Cambridge: MIT Press.

——— 1986. *The "uncensored war": The media and Vietnam.* New York: Oxford Univ. Press.

Hallin, D. C., and P. Mancini. 1984. Speaking of the president: Political structure and representational form in U.S. and Italian television news. *Theory and Society* 13:829–50.

Hamill, R., T. D. Wilson, and R. E. Nisbett. 1980. Insensitivity to sample bias: Generalizing from atypical cases. *Journal of Personality and Social Psychology* 39:578–89.

Hansen, J. M., and S. J. Rosenstone. 1984. Context, mobilization, and political participation. Paper delivered at the Weingart Conference on Institutional Context of Elections, California Institute of Technology, Pasadena.

Hanushek, E., and J. Jackson. 1977. *Statistical methods for social scientists.* New York: Academic Press.

Hendricks, J. S., and W. M. Denney. 1979. Energy, inflation, and economic discontents: A study of citizen understanding and response. Progress report, The Center for Energy Studies, The Univ. of Texas at Austin.

Hibbs, D. A., Jr. 1977. Political parties and macroeconomic performance. *American Political Science Review* 71:1467–87.

Hibbs, D. A., Jr., D. Rivers, and N. Vasilatos. 1982a. On the demand for economic outcomes: Macroeconomic performance and mass political support in the United States, Great Britain, and Germany. *Journal of Politics* 44: 426–62.

——— 1982b. The dynamics of political support for American presidents among occupational and partisan groups. *American Journal of Political Science* 26:312–32.

Higgins, E. T., and G. King. 1981. Accessibility of social constructs: Information-processing consequences of individual and contextual variability. In *Personality, cognition, and social interactions*, ed. by N. Cantor and J. Kihlstrom. Hillsdale, N.J.: Erlbaum.

Higgins, E. T., W. S. Rholes, and C. R. Jones. 1977. Category accessibility and impression formation. *Journal of Experimental Social Psychology* 13: 141–54.

Hofstetter, C. R. 1976. *Bias in the news.* Columbus: Ohio State Univ. Press.

Hovland, C. I. 1959. Reconciling conflicting results derived from experimental and survey studies of attitude change. *American Psychologist* 14:8–17.

Hovland, C. I., A. Lumsdaine, and F. Sheffield. 1949. *Experiments on mass communication.* Princeton: Princeton Univ. Press.

Huntington, S. P. 1975. The United States. In *The crisis of democracy*, ed. by M. Crozier, S. P. Huntington, and J. Watanuki. New York: New York Univ. Press.

Iyengar, S. 1979. Television news and issue salience. *American Politics Quarterly* 7:395–416.

Iyengar, S., and D. R. Kinder. 1986a. Psychological accounts of agenda-setting. In *Mass media and political thought*, ed. by S. Kraus and R. Perloff. Beverly Hills: Sage.

——— 1986b. More than meets the eye: TV news, priming, and presidential evaluations. Vol. 1, in *Public communication and behavior*, ed. by G. Comstock. New York: Academic Press.

Iyengar, S., D. R. Kinder, M. D. Peters, and J. A. Krosnick. 1984. The evening news and presidential evaluations. *Journal of Personality and Social Psychology* 46:778–87.

Jacobson, G. C. 1981. Incumbents' advantages in the 1978 U.S. Congressional elections. *Legislative Studies Quarterly* 6:183–200.

Johnston, J. 1972. *Econometric methods.* New York: McGraw Hill.

Kahneman, D., and A. Tversky. 1979. Prospect theory: An analysis of decision under risk. *Econometrica* 47:263–91.

———— 1984. Choices, values and frames. *American Psychologist* 39:341–50.

Kelley, H. H. 1972. *Causal schemata and the attribution process.* Morristown, N.J.: General Learning Press.

———— 1973. The processes of causal attribution. *American Psychologist* 28:107–28.

Kernell, S. 1978. Explaining presidential popularity. *American Political Science Review* 72:506–22.

———— 1986. *Going public.* Washington, D.C.: Congressional Quarterly Press.

Key, V. O., Jr. 1961. *Public opinion and American democracy.* New York: Knopf.

Kiewiet, D. R. 1983. *Macroeconomics and micropolitics: The electoral effects of economic issues.* Chicago: Univ. of Chicago Press.

Kinder, D. R. 1983. Diversity and complexity in American public opinion. In *The state of the discipline,* ed. by A. Finifter. Washington, D.C.: APSA.

———— 1985. Presidential character revisited. In *Cognition and political behavior,* ed. by R. Lau and D. O. Sears. Hillsdale, N.J.: Erlbaum.

Kinder, D. R., and Abelson, R. P. 1981. Appraising presidential candidates: Personality and affect in the 1980 campaign. Paper delivered at the Annual Meeting of the American Political Science Association, New York City.

Kinder, D. R., G. S. Adams, and P. W. Gronke. 1985. Economics and politics in 1984. Paper delivered at the Annual Meeting of the American Political Science Association, New Orleans.

Kinder, D. R., and D. R. Kiewiet. 1979. Economic discontent and political behavior: The role of personal grievances and collective economic judgments in congressional voting. *American Journal of Political Science* 23: 495–527.

————. 1981. Sociotropic politics. *British Journal of Political Science* 11: 129–61.

Kinder, D. R., and W. R. Mebane, Jr. 1983. Politics and economics in everyday life. *The political process and economic change,* ed. by K. Monroe. New York: Agathon Press.

Kinder, D. R., and L. A. Rhodebeck. 1982. Continuities in support for racial equality, 1972 to 1976. *Public Opinion Quarterly* 46:195–215.

Kinder, D. R., and D. O. Sears. 1981. Prejudice and politics: Symbolic racism versus racial threats to the good life. *Journal of Personality and Social Psychology* 40:414–31.

———— 1985. Public opinion and political behavior. Vol. 2, in *Handbook of social psychology,* 3d ed., ed. by G. Lindzey and E. Aronson. New York: Random House.

Kingdon, J. W. 1984. *Agendas, alternatives, and public policies.* Boston: Little Brown.

Klapper, J. 1960. *The effects of mass communications.* New York: Free Press.

Kramer, G. H. 1971. Short-term fluctuations in U.S. voting behavior, 1896–1964. *American Political Science Review* 65:131–43.

Lane, R. E. 1978. Interpersonal relations and leadership in a "cold society." *Comparative Politics* 10:443–59.

Lau, R. R., T. A. Brown, and D. O. Sears. 1978. Self-interest and civilians' attitudes toward the Vietnam War. *Public Opinion Quarterly* 42:464–83.

Lazarsfeld, P. F., B. Berelson, and H. Gaudet. 1948. *The people's choice,* 2d ed. New York: Columbia Univ. Press.

Lazarsfeld, P. F., and R. K. Merton. 1948. Mass communication, popular taste, and organized social action. In *The communication of ideas,* ed. by L. Bryson. New York: Harper.

Lindblom, C. E. 1977. *Politics and markets.* New York: Basic Books.

Lippmann, W. 1920. *Liberty and the news.* New York: Harcourt, Brace, and Howe.

———— 1922. *Public opinion.* New York: Macmillan.

———— 1925. *The phantom public.* New York: Harcourt Brace Jovanovich.

McCombs, M. E. 1981. The agenda-setting approach. In *Handbook of political communication,* ed. by D. D. Nimmo and K. R. Sanders. Beverly Hills: Sage.

McCombs, M. E., and D. Shaw. 1972. The agenda-setting function of the mass media. *Public Opinion Quarterly* 36:176–87.

McConnell, G. 1966. *Private power and American democracy.* New York: Random House.

McGuire, W. J. 1968. Personality and susceptibility to social influence. In *Handbook of personality theory and research,* ed. by E F. Borgatta and W. W. Lambert. Chicago: Rand McNally.

———— 1985. Attitudes and attitude change. Vol. 2, in *The handbook of social psychology,* 3d ed., ed. by G. Lindzey and E. Aronson. New York: Random House.

MacKuen, M. 1981. Social communication and the mass policy agenda. In *More than news: media power in public affairs,* ed. by M. MacKuen and S. L. Coombs, 19–144. Beverly Hills: Sage.

———— 1983. Political drama, economic conditions, and the dynamics of presidential popularity. *American Journal of Political Science* 27:165–92.

———— 1984. Exposure to information, belief integration, and individual responsiveness to agenda change. *American Political Science Review* 78:372–91.

Mann, T. E. 1978. *Unsafe at any margin: Interpreting congressional elections.* Washington, D.C.: American Enterprise Institute.

Mann, T. E., and R. E. Wolfinger. 1980. Candidates and parties in congressional elections. *American Political Science Review* 74:617–32.

Markus, G. B. 1979. *Analyzing panel data.* Beverly Hills: Sage.

Matthews, D. R. 1978. "Winnowing": The news media and the 1976 presidential nominations. In *Race for the presidency,* ed. by J. D. Barber. Englewood Cliffs, N.J.: Prentice-Hall.

Mayhew, D. R. 1974. *Congress: The electoral connection.* New Haven: Yale Univ. Press.

Miller, A. H., P. Gurin, G. Gurin, and O. Malanchuk. 1981. Group consciousness and political participation. *American Journal of Political Science* 25: 494–511.

Miller, A. H., and W. E. Miller. 1976. Ideology in the 1972 election: Myth and reality. *American Political Science Review* 70:832–49.

Neustadt, R. E. 1960. *Presidential power: The politics of leadership.* New York: Wiley.

Nisbett, R. E., and L. Ross. 1980. *Human inference: Strategies and shortcomings of social judgment.* Englewood Cliffs, N.J.: Prentice-Hall.

Nisbett, R. E., and T. D. Wilson. 1977. Telling more than we can know: Verbal reports on mental processes. *Psychological Review* 84:231–59.

Oberdorfer, D. 1971. *Tet!* New York: Doubleday & Co.

Orne, M. T. 1962. On the social psychology of the psychological experiment: With particular reference to demand characteristics and their implications. *American Psychologist* 17:776–83.

Ostrom, C. W., and D. M. Simon, Jr. 1985. Promise and performance: A dynamic model of presidential popularity. *American Political Science Review* 79:334–58.

Page, B. I. 1978. *Choices and echoes in presidential elections.* Chicago: Univ. of Chicago Press.

Page, B. I., and R. P. Shapiro. 1983. Effects of public opinion on policy. *American Political Science Review* 77:175–90.

Patterson, T. 1980. *The mass media election: How Americans choose their president.* New York: Praeger.

Patterson, T., and R. McClure. 1976. *The unseeing eye: The myth of television power in national elections.* New York: G. P. Putnam.

Polsby, N. 1983. *Consequences of party reform.* New York: Oxford Univ. Press.

Popkin, S., J. W. Gorman, C. Phillips, and J. A. Smith. 1976. Comment: What have you done for me lately? Toward an investment theory of voting. *American Political Science Review* 70:779–805.

Postman, N. 1985. *Amusing ourselves to death.* New York: Viking.

Public Opinion. 1981. A conversation with the President's Pollsters—Patrick Caddell and Richard Wirthlin. *Public Opinion* 3 (Dec./Jan.): 2–12, 63–64.

Ranney, A. 1983. *Channels of power.* New York: Basic Books.

Rivers, D., and N. L. Rose. 1985. Passing the president's program: Public opinion and presidential influence in Congress. *American Journal of Political Science* 29:183–96.

Robinson, M. J. 1976a. Public affairs television and the growth of political malaise: The case of "the selling of the Pentagon." *American Political Science Review* 70:409–32.

——— 1976b. American political legitimacy in an era of electronic journalism: Reflections on the evening news. In *Television as a social force: New approaches to TV criticism,* ed. by D. Cater and R. Adler. New York: Praeger.

——— 1977. Television and American politics. *The Public Interest* 48:3–39.

Robinson, M. J., and M. A. Sheehan. 1983. *Over the wire and on TV*. New York: Russell Sage.

Rosenberg, S. 1977. New approaches to the analysis of personal constructs in person perception. Vol. 24, in *Nebraska Symposium on Motivation*, ed. by D. Levine. Lincoln: Nebraska Univ. Press.

Rothman, S. 1980. The mass media in post-industrial society. In *The third century: America as a post-industrial society*, ed. by S. M. Lipset. Stanford, Calif.: Hoover Institution Press.

Rubin, R. L. 1981. *Press, party, and presidency*. New York: W. W. Norton.

Rubin, Z. 1973. *Liking and loving*. New York: Holt, Rinehart and Winston.

Schandler, H. 1977. *The unmaking of a president*. Princeton: Princeton Univ. Press.

Schattschneider, E. E. 1960. *The semi-sovereign people*. New York: Holt.

Schudson, M. 1978. *Discovering the news*. New York: Basic Books.

Schuman, H. 1973. The sources of anti-war sentiment in America. *American Journal of Sociology* 78:513–36.

Schuman, H., and S. Presser. 1981. *Questions and answers in attitude surveys: Experiments on question form, wording, and context*. New York: Academic Press.

Sears, D. O., and S. Chaffee. 1979. Uses and effects of the 1976 debates: An overview of empirical studies. In *The great debates, 1976: Ford vs. Carter*, ed. by S. Kraus. Bloomington: Indiana Univ. Press.

Sears, D. O., and J. Citrin. 1982. *Tax revolt: Something for nothing in California*. Cambridge: Harvard Univ. Press.

Sears, D. O., T. R. Tyler, T. Citrin, and D. R. Kinder. 1978. Political system support and public response to the energy crisis. *American Journal of Political Science* 22:56–82.

Sears, D. O., and R. E. Whitney. 1973. Political persuasion. In *Handbook of communication*, ed. by I. Pool, W. Schramm, F. W. Frey, N. Maccoby, and E. B. Parker. Chicago: Rand McNally.

Sigal, L. V. 1973. *Reporters and officials*. Lexington, Mass.: D. C. Heath.

Simon, H. A. 1955. A behavioral model of rational choice. *Quarterly Journal of Economics* 69:99–118.

——— 1979. *Models of thought*. New Haven: Yale Univ. Press.

Srull, T. K., and R. S. Wyer. 1979. The role of category accessibility in the interpretation of information about persons: Some determinants and implications. *Journal of Personality and Social Psychology* 37:1160–72.

Stokes, D. E. 1966. Party loyalty and the likelihood of deviating elections. In *Elections and the political order*, ed. by A. Campbell, P. E. Converse, W. E. Miller, and D. E. Stokes. New York: Wiley.

Stokes, D. E., and Miller, W. E. 1962. Party government and the salience of Congress. *Public Opinion Quarterly* 26:19–28.

Taylor, S., and S. Thompson. 1982. Stalking the elusive "vividness" effect. *Psychological Review* 89:155–81.

Tuchman, G. 1972. Objectivity as strategic ritual: An examination of newsmen's notions of objectivity. *American Journal of Sociology* 77:660–79.

Tufte, E. R. 1978. *Political control of the economy.* Princeton: Princeton Univ. Press.

Turner, C. F., and Krauss, E. 1978. Fallible indicators of the subjective state of the nation. *American Psychologist* 33:456–70.

Tversky, A., and D. Kahneman. 1974. Judgment under uncertainty: Heuristics and biases. *Science* 185:1124–31.

——— 1981. The framing of decisions and the psychology of choice. *Science* 211:453–58.

Tyler, T. R. 1980. Impact of directly and indirectly experienced events: The origins of crime-related judgments and behaviors. *Journal of Personality and Social Psychology* 39:13–28.

Verba, S., and N. H. Nie. 1972. *Participation in America: Political democracy and social equality.* Chicago: Harper & Row.

Weaver, D. H., D. Graber, M. E. McCombs, and C. H. Eyal. 1981. *Media agenda-setting in a presidential election.* New York: Praeger.

Weaver, P. H. 1972. Is television news biased? *The Public Interest* 26:57–74.

——— 1975. Newspaper news and television news. In *Television as social force: New approaches to TV criticism,* ed. by D. Cater and R. Adler. New York: Praeger.

Weissberg, R. 1976. *Public opinion and popular government.* Englewood Cliffs, N.J.: Prentice-Hall.

Winkler, R. L., and W. L. Hays. 1975. *Statistics, probability, inference, and decision.* New York: Holt, Rinehart, and Winston.

Wise, S. 1979. Big story. *Journal of Politics* 41:1223–26.

Zaller, J. 1986. The diffusion of political attitudes. *Journal of Personality and Social Psychology,* in press.

Index